Invisible Ink

Invisible Ink

NAVIGATING RACISM IN CORPORATE AMERICA

● ● ●

Stephen M. Graham

**The notable difference between black
excellence and white excellence is that
white excellence is achieved without
having to battle racism. Imagine.[i]**

—CLAUDIA RANKINE

With a foreword by Jim Sinegal, cofounder and former
CEO of Costco Wholesale Corporation

---

i From Claudia Rankine, "The Meaning of Serena Williams," *New
York Times Magazine*, August 30, 2015.

ISBN-13: 9781541171176
ISBN-10: 1541171179
Library of Congress Control Number: 2016920965
CreateSpace Independent Publishing Platform
North Charleston, South Carolina

To Joanne
The love of my life

Author's Note

● ● ●

To CAPTURE EXAMPLES OF THE many forms of bias and racism in corporate America, their effects, how one bearing the brunt might respond, how one wanting to effect change might respond, and how one practiced in denial might respond, I have simply described many of my experiences and left the reader to draw his or her own conclusions as to lessons learned or insights gained. In other words, my intent is to provoke thought and introspection. In so doing, I have tried to steer clear of lecturing or focusing on incidents that, to my mind, clearly involved racism but, as is so often the case, left me with little more than circumstantial evidence to support my conclusions. In short, I have painted a picture of racism in America, and it is up to the reader to find meaning in that picture or not. And certainly, one will find little meaning, little ability to communicate effectively, little understanding of how their actions may be perceived, little ability to cross the divide and effect change, without appreciating the whole picture and how all of its pieces are interconnected, each impacting the whole.

I have had the good fortune to have spent my legal career with three of the finest law firms in the world: Perkins Coie, where it all began, followed by Orrick and Fenwick & West. As noted on the pages that follow, there were times when certain individuals associated with those firms behaved in less-than-exemplary fashion when it came to bias, be it in expressing their own or in standing up to the bias of others. The actions of these individuals, however, reflect what is typical in corporate American and should not be used to diminish any firm as an institution. Indeed, each firm gave me a shot and enabled me to reach a level of prominence in my profession that had in no way been guaranteed. This is the important fact, not the fact that each institution happened to be populated by imperfect human beings, I, of course, being one. In this regard, it is also important to remember that, while its levels and intensity may vary, bias is everywhere. But goodwill is everywhere, too, which should inspire those challenged by racism to stay the course.

In retelling many of the stories that appear in this book, I have used dialogue to describe conversations, although recapturing exact quotes from conversations that were not recorded is, of course, not entirely possible.

Also, please note that to avoid the stilted "he or she" and "his or her" convention, where appropriate, I alternate the use of masculine and feminine pronouns.

Foreword

• • •

IN THE EARLY SPRING OF this year, I stopped by a local car wash to get the winter grime off my vehicle. At the end of the process, I spotted my transformed car, which now looked as if it were fresh off the showroom floor, and I approached a young Latino man standing near it, assuming he was part of the detailing crew. I prepared to hand him a tip. Fortunately for me, before I had a chance to embarrass myself, the young man got into the car behind mine, started his engine, and drove away. I felt temporarily shamed by my stupid assumption but quickly got over it and went on with my day. I didn't give the experience, or the way in which the "innocent" bias ingrained in our society adversely affects the lives of minorities every minute of every day, a second thought. That is, not until I read *Invisible Ink*.

I began to realize that through the years, I had failed to honestly confront my own ingrained bias, allowing myself to fall into the convenient trap of deeming myself unbiased by virtue of my open mind. I reflected on the many times my insensitive actions had likely caused offense, such as the time when, leaving the El Gaucho restaurant in downtown Seattle, I tried to give my valet check to a black man who was also waiting for his car. And I began to think of those business decisions, on my part and on the part of my colleagues, that in retrospect might have been driven by bias, unconscious or otherwise.

When Steve Graham approached me about writing a foreword for *Invisible Ink*, I asked, "Why me?" After all, what did I know about navigating racism in corporate America? His response was, "Well, you are one of the most successful businessmen in the country, and I would be interested in your perspective. Does my story matter? In your view, does institutional racism in corporate America remain a significant issue? Is it important for business leaders to more readily acknowledge bias and more fully appreciate its cumulative effect on the careers of minorities and to take more meaningful steps to do something about it?" I agreed to review the draft manuscript and offer my comments.

After about five or six chapters, my initial reaction was, *Wow, this guy is really sensitive and a bit of a whiner! Get a grip!* As I moved further into the narrative, my attitude changed completely. It was now, *Holy shit! How does a person put up with this?* His is a classic example of "death by a thousand cuts." How do people not just give up? How do they control their hurt and anger?

Now I was asking the question "Why me?" a second time, but from a different viewpoint. It became clear to me that I am personally part of a problem that is one of the most, if not the most, complicated and concealed in our society. No, I really do not believe that I'm racist, but why so many transgressions? Why so many subtle and inadvertent slights? Why, when I followed the careers of my two favorite basketball players, Magic Johnson and Larry Bird, did I always look to see which one had scored the most points or came closest to a "triple double," and why did I always hope it was Larry, even though I loved both players? I clearly loved Bird just a little bit more despite the fact that the Lakers are my cherished team.

I'm eighty years old and grew up in a time when the prevailing view was that a black man could never be smart enough to quarterback an NFL team. Arguably, the underlying racism that produced that kind of thinking is no longer a significant issue. After all, we elected an African American as president of our country, the most powerful position in the world. Yet he is insulted with impunity during a State of the Union address by a congressman screaming out, "You lie!" The only word he omitted was "boy." Is bias toward African Americans and other minorities in corporate America no longer a significant issue? Far from it. And one reason that our race problem persists is our steadfast refusal to truly and honestly confront our past and the present-day products of that past.

About a year ago, a good friend of mine asked a mutual African American friend the question, "Do you ever feel discriminated against?" Our African American friend, with whom we had worked for thirty years, would be the last guy in the world I would have expected to have been burdened by racism. He looked my other friend in the eye and said, "Every day of my life."

I am certain that many African Americans, Latinos, and Native Americans are now asking, "How long has this guy Sinegal been drinking the Kool-Aid?" Saying "I'm not prejudiced" is comparable to Richard Nixon's "I am not a crook" assertion. I may not be an overt racist, but I cannot claim to have been part of the solution. I have witnessed, without seeing, countless acts of racism down through the years, both in corporate America as well as in the larger society. I'm as guilty as anyone of unrecognized bias and inadvertent slights. Though innocent and small, the cumulative effect of those slights, especially when multiplied to account for what happens in the larger society, boggles the mind. We simply do not give enough thought to bias and its consequences, often paying little more than lip service to the issues that exist. My thanks to Steve Graham, because after reading *Invisible Ink*, I intend to do whatever I can to change that.

Jim Sinegal
Cofounder and former CEO of
Costco Wholesale Corporation

Prologue

● ● ●

IT HAS ALWAYS BEEN AN uphill struggle for the relatively few African Americans in corporate America who do exist, and it is made all the more difficult because we tend to operate in isolation. We are nearly always alone, with no one to fall back on when we stumble or get punched in the gut as we deal daily with an unending stream of slights real and imagined. Even those who do care don't really understand. This is all played out in an environment where we are continuously subjected to a debilitating undercurrent of bias that too many, on both sides of the divide, pretend does not exist.

A Yale law degree provides little comfort. No matter what I accomplish, I will always be a black man and prejudged accordingly, consciously or subconsciously. In fact, a Yale degree may in some ways intensify my frustration in that it has always magnified the disconnect between how I believe I should be treated and how I am actually treated, the gap between the respect I think I have earned and the disrespect often accorded simply due to the color of my skin.

At times over the years, I have felt like throwing in the towel. The subtle put-downs, the dismissive behavior, the slights, intended and unintended, the inability to secure work given to those half as bright but colored white. The discrimination and the subtle indignities that must be endured by all minorities trying to succeed in corporate America are constant. For any African American wishing to be seen in this environment as an equal and not to be seen, if at all, as a nameless, faceless ink spot at odds with the landscape, the road can be tough.

Admittedly, succeeding in corporate America is difficult for most everyone. For African Americans, however, succeeding takes hard work and determination at levels seldom understood by, and certainly not required of, white participants, as we are forced to battle racism at every turn, within and without our organizations, while using whatever energy remains to strive for, and actually achieve, excellence in our chosen fields. It wears you down. It can make you physically ill. It can paralyze your mind. You want to quit, aching from the pain but trying to hold on just one more day with the hope that things will get better. The temptation to succumb to fatigue and feelings of self-doubt are reminders that, although seldom allowed to be, we are in fact human. But we soldier on, actually becoming stronger in the process, subscribing to the motto that they can kill us, but we are not going to kill ourselves.

We do perform a balancing act as we pretend, along with everyone else, that all is well. We bottle up our feelings, not wanting to be the angry black man or woman and knowing that we wouldn't be understood anyway. This is not healthy, and in the end, it will not prolong our survival in this world, but it is our reality.

Definitions

● ● ●

Racism: A BELIEF OR DOCTRINE that inherent differences among various human races determine cultural or individual achievement, usually involving the idea that one's own race is superior. The belief that all members of each race possess characteristics or abilities specific to that race, especially so as to distinguish it as inferior or superior to another race or races.

Bigotry: A state of mind in which a person views other groups with fear, distrust, prejudice, or hatred solely on the basis of ethnicity, race, religion, gender, etc.

Bias: Prejudice, usually unfair, in favor of or against one thing, person, or group compared to another.

Confirmation Bias: A mental shortcut built into the brain that makes one actively seek information, interpretation, and memory that only observes and absorbs what affirms established beliefs while ignoring data that contradicts those beliefs.

Explicit Bias: The attitudes and beliefs we have about a person or a group at the conscious level.

Implicit Bias: The bias in judgment or behavior that results from subtle cognitive processes that often operate at a level below conscious awareness.

Context

● ● ●

A WHITE MAN MAKES A purchase in a grocery store, handing a twenty-dollar bill to the white cashier. The man holds out his hand to receive his change. The cashier places the change on the counter. The man picks up his change and leaves the store, never giving it a second thought.

Same scenario, only now the man is an African American: for him, it is more complicated. As he stands there with his empty hand outstretched, staring at the change on the counter, he is left to wonder,[1] *Does the cashier know what she just did? Did she mean anything by it? Was her action motivated by racism, if only subconsciously? Or was this all very innocent?* A black person too often is simply left to wonder. In corporate America, each time an e-mail

---

1 During the segregation era in the United States, one of the ways in which African Americans were demeaned was by the prohibition of physical contact between the races. When a black person purchased something from a white person in a store, the exchange of money was made on the counter so that white hands would not be "dirtied" by touching black hands. Add this to the list of other indignities blacks were forced to endure daily, and it takes on even greater symbolic significance.

goes unanswered, an overture is rejected, a comment is interrupted, an invitation is not received, a condescending comment is made, an instruction is ignored, a pitch is lost, an opportunity is diverted, a black person is simply left to wonder.

CHAPTER 1

Why?

● ● ●

I DECIDED TO WRITE THIS book primarily for four reasons.

First, I write as a counter to all the pretending. Too many white people pretend that bias does not exist in corporate America or that, if it does, it certainly has no appreciable negative effect on the lives and careers of African Americans—not today.[2] They are joined by those blind to bias, their own as well as that of others.[3] Their accomplices in maintaining this fantasyland, and thus the status quo, are the African Americans who, as a survival mechanism, pretend that, while bias exists, they are not affected by it.

---

2   Throughout my career I have had to deal with racial bias and throughout my career too many of those around me have denied its existence – year in and year out, decade in and decade out. What was said twenty years ago concerning corporate America is the same that is said today – there may have been racial bias yesterday, but not today. So we have a kind of rolling admission that always lags behind the present.

3 In "Disrespect, Race and Obama," his November 16, 2013, *New York Times* op-ed, Charles M. Blow writes, "Race consciousness is real. Racial assumptions and prejudices are real. And racism is real. But these realities can operate without articulation and beneath awareness." It is this fact that makes denial easy and eradication difficult.

They foolishly believe that they have risen above it all, because no one calls them niggers to their faces. To admit
otherwise would surely be seen as a sign of weakness or
claiming victimhood or being difficult—or, worse, playing the race card.

My second reason for writing this book was to bring
to life and out of the shadows what too many see as an
almost abstract notion—namely, the constant stream of
racism that African Americans must endure throughout
their lives as they struggle to compete and to maintain
self-esteem, focus, and sanity in a society dominated by
those who just cannot seem to accept them as their equals,
not completely. This steady drip, drip, with the occasional
barrage, is neither abstract nor anonymous. It is real, and it
is personal. And it takes its toll. It may not be as dramatic
as violent criminal behavior, but it is more widespread, and
the damage inflicted on the African American community
is infinitely greater. Similarly, a hostile work environment
doesn't require the placement of a noose on an African
American's desk. All it takes is the failure of his colleagues
to vigorously oppose insensitive conduct or even acknowledge it, brushing it off as inconsequential or ignoring it
altogether.

My third reason for writing this book was to send a
message to other African Americans, especially those beginning their careers, that they are not alone, that there are
others who understand and share in this struggle, and that
none of us are immune—not even those of us fortunate

enough to have Ivy League degrees and positions in the nation's top corporations, law firms, and other organizations. We have transcended the worst that America has had to offer and have taken advantage of the best, but it remains a struggle.

And, finally, I have written this book to help provoke awareness and appreciation of the ingrained bias working to undermine fairness at every level of our society, with the hope that this will result in greater acknowledgment and understanding of some of the darker threads woven into the fabric of America. Without acknowledgment, discussion, and understanding, we are doomed to repeat past mistakes and doomed to fail in our efforts to correct our most significant social ills. If we choose to excuse our past rather than confront it (as did Germany in the context of the Holocaust), if we choose tolerance over acceptance, if we choose politeness over understanding, if we choose fantasy over reality, no matter how well intentioned, we are choosing to remain sick as a nation.

As a society, we continue to suffer from the lingering effects of slavery and Jim Crow and that post–Jim Crow period, whatever you might want to call it, when people stopped saying bad things but didn't stop doing them. A great many people in positions of power and influence, white and black, act on subconscious bias (if not conscious bias), rejecting African Americans as their equals or as the equal of an equally (or less) qualified white individual. Or, even if not biased themselves, they reject anyway, just to be safe, based on what they think someone else might be thinking.[4] This is the reality.

I once heard a black television commentator say that he had never had a negative encounter with a white policeman. I wondered what rock he had just crawled out from under. Similarly, I read where a black kid attending an Ivy League school said that he didn't see any disadvantage associated with being African American. My thought was that he had learned his lines well and that he should test his conclusions late one night on the South Side of Chicago, where bias can be a little less subtle.

Ignoring reality, while making us feel better about ourselves in the near term, never helps anything in the long term. This is not to suggest that we should dwell on the negative, because we should not. We must be aware, however, if understanding, change, and fairness are to be

---

4 Some women and minorities believe that advocating on behalf of their particular affinity group can be a liability in the workplace. Researchers found that "women and nonwhite executives who push for women and nonwhites to be hired and promoted suffer when it comes to their own performance reviews. A woman who shepherds women up the ranks, for example, is perceived as less warm, while a nonwhite who promotes diversity is perceived as less competent...often, having women or minorities atop a company is perceived as a marker for progress for diversity efforts, but Dr. [David] Hekman's research suggests their presence might not have a large impact on the rest of the organization. If they believe it is too risky to advocate for their own groups, it makes sense that successful women and nonwhite leaders would end up surrounded by white males in the executive suite." The truly perverse finding is that white men actually received a bump in their performance review scores from valuing diversity. Rachel Feintzeig, "Study Finds Diversity Toll," *Wall Street Journal*, July 24, 2014.

achieved. We need to own up to the fact that bias exists and that it has undermined and continues to undermine the lives and careers of African Americans – then we actually have to do something about it. It is not enough for the white partner to note that the African American associate is affected by bias – he must actually do something to counter it – something more than attending the annual Black History Month lunch.

Many African Americans, myself included, have at times wrongly concluded that if we are quiet about it, perhaps "they" will forget that we are black, thereby contributing to our own invisibility and lending support to racist notions. We believed that accomplishment would inoculate us against explicit bias, perhaps even implicit bias, and we would be off and running with our careers, happily leaving racism in our wake. Wishful thinking. Decades ago, I blasted off with my career, but I only managed to achieve high orbit, never quite escaping racism's gravitational pull. Over time, I have been forced to admit that no matter what I accomplish, for far too many, I will always be first an African American man and, as such, consistent with the messaging firmly embedded in the fabric of our society, someone to fear, target, despise, dismiss, and/or disrespect, virtually never someone to truly embrace, to accept as an equal without equivocation.[5] We are closing the gap in terms of race relations

---

5 This understanding is a thread that runs throughout our society on both sides of the divide. It is just expressed in different ways and in the

– today is much different than yesterday – so we think we have arrived. Because we interview African Americans when opportunities present themselves, mimicking the Rooney Rule in professional football[6], we deem all is well, ignoring the frequency with which the African American does not get the assignment. We have replaced overt racism with charades. Progress?

---

final analysis means different things, depending on one's point of view. When Jackie Robinson joined the Brooklyn Dodgers, the manager of the Philadelphia Phillies, Ben Chapman, is reported to have said to him, "Jackie, you know, you're a good ballplayer, but you're still a nigger to me." Once as I walked down a Seattle street, I was approached by a black man panhandling. He asked me whether I would give him some money. Consistent with my policy, I said no. He was indignant, and in response, he yelled at me, "You're still a nigger!" It is the same sentiment expressed much more subtly by many whites toward upwardly mobile African Americans, unless of course you are a congressman yelling out to the president of the United States during a State of the Union speech, "You lie!" In that same vein, once, as I sat with several white men waiting for a board of directors meeting to begin, one of the directors recounted something that had appeared in the paper about a misstep by the CEO of another company (who happened to be an African American). The director referred to the CEO not by name and not as "that CEO," but as "that black CEO."

6 The Rooney Rule is a National Football League policy that requires league teams to interview minority candidates for head coaching and senior football operations positions. As in too much of corporate America, the resulting respect accorded African Americans is often feigned. While no longer completely ignored, African Americans are now interviewed but seldom seriously considered. NFL teams have taken a chance on twenty-one first-time white head coaches and only one first-time minority head coach over the past five hiring cycles (2012-2016). The gap was an identical 21-1 twenty years ago.

And sometimes, instead of being replaced, the overt racism takes on a quasi-overt form, in that instead of someone remarking to your face, using a loud whisper, a racist comment is made to another – the comment is not directed to you, but it is clearly intended for your benefit. I have seen this technique employed by opposing counsel and at least one venture capitalist.

Despite the challenges I have faced due solely to the color of my skin, I have achieved a significant measure of success: Yale Law School; three major law firm partnerships, opening offices for two;[7] a seven-figure income. So where's the bias, one might ask? Those who ask fail to appreciate that I did not achieve success because of the absence of bias but in spite of its existence. I was strong enough, with

---

7 I opened Seattle offices for Orrick in 2000 and Fenwick & West in 2008. Both ventures were successful, in significant part due to the presence of two colleagues who were with me every step of the way: Alan Smith and Ellen Welichko. Alan and I have worked together from the day he joined Perkins Coie to begin his law firm career, and Ellen, a senior corporate legal assistant, and I have worked together for more than thirty years. If Alan (who has since become my partner) and Ellen had not chosen to leave Perkins to follow me to Orrick, there's a good chance I'd have failed. I had never tried to build a law office from the ground up before and did not fully appreciate the need for a solid core composed of more than one individual to serve as a foundation. Both Alan and Ellen are brilliant in their own right, and their contributions have been absolutely essential. They could have taken the safe route and stayed at Perkins, but they came with me. I love them and owe them a debt of gratitude for their faith, courage, loyalty, and friendship.

the help of some well-timed mentoring[8] and a core group of fiercely loyal clients willing to accept me not only as an individual but also as a competent professional, to absorb the punches and meet the challenges. I refused to quit, and I survived. Moreover, the true measure is what I could have achieved had I been supported as readily as I have sometimes been dismissed and nudged aside. While President Obama's accomplishments as president are significant, imagine what he could have accomplished if the powers aligned against him had chosen to instead collaborate.

Over the years, I have had conversations with white colleagues that have gone something like this:

---

8 No one does it alone. Throughout history, there have always been people of goodwill whose minds and hearts are more open and whose level of courage is much greater than that of most who are willing to step in and work against the grain to make a difference. I will be forever indebted to the following individuals who stood beside me when others did not: Alston J. Shakeshaft, my college advisor who guided me to Yale Law School; Guido Calabresi, who helped me find my way at Yale; David Wagoner, the Perkins Coie partner who interviewed me at Yale and made sure I got a shot at a corporate law firm career; and Tom Alberg, the Perkins Coie partner who took me under his wing and stood against my detractors, cutting a trip to New York short so that he could return to Seattle and argue for my partnership in front of the executive committee, some members of which had vowed never to make me a partner. Most recently, Gordy Davidson, as chairman of Fenwick & West, sought me out to join Fenwick and begin an office in Seattle – obviously a rare and significant opportunity. At the other end of the spectrum are the youngsters, those bright young men and women coming out of law school well after me who, unlike so many other white individuals, readily accepted my leadership and had my back, not seeing race, at least not in a negative light. This generation is led by my current right hand man, Andy Albertson, who continues to set new standards of excellence.

Me:	You do acknowledge that racism has long been a feature of American society?
White Colleague:	Yes.
Me:	You do understand that African Americans have suffered the brunt of American racism?
WC:	Yes.
Me:	You do realize that racism still exists?
WC:	Yes.
Me:	You do know that I am an African American?
WC:	Well, yes, now that you mention it.
Me:	Do you really believe that when I am being assessed by white business-people, when pitching for business or otherwise competing, that I stand on a level playing field?
WC:	Perhaps not all of the time.
Me:	Well, when it comes to career advancement or winning business from white men and women, do you really believe that no decision involving my hiring or advancement has ever been driven by racism?
WC:	No.
Me:	What percentage of the time were they?
WC:	I have no idea.

Me: Neither do I. That's the fun part! We know it's there, but most of the time, we are just left to wonder. Seldom are we confronted with overt bias. Today's racism is subtle, implicit, sneaky,[9] rendering denial easy. But it is always there, even if existing only in the form of a threat or a possibility.

WC: You have a point.

I am left with the impression that the white colleague feels uneasy in these exchanges, but the unease quickly dissipates once he is out of my presence. Then it's back to business as usual.

Racism, of course, covers a broad spectrum of attitudes and behaviors. One end is occupied by those who are accepting, wouldn't think twice about living next door, and comply with all the rules associated with polite society but who still see black and think negative, even if only subconsciously. The uglier type of racism is, by and large, relegated to the fringe and, though obnoxious (and dangerous), is not a significant practical problem today in corporate America (although, shockingly, it still rears its head from time to time, often when alcohol is involved).

---

9 Charles M. Blow notes in "Disrespect, Race and Obama" that "racism is a virus that is growing clever at avoiding detection."

The "polite" form of racism, however, is in many ways just as harmful as the more socially obnoxious form and just as lethal in terms of undermining African American economic success and inflicting lasting damage to the psyche. It is the racism that every hour of every day operates to rob African Americans of opportunities and stifle their careers, if only in barely perceptible increments.[10] The resulting compounded economic loss to African American households is absolutely staggering. A nonviolent death is still a death.

Three hundred years of inculcating into the collective American subconscious the ideas that African Americans are property, subhuman, savage, and stupid (just for openers) has had, not surprisingly, a lingering negative effect. Overt racism may be reduced or in some cases eliminated, but the residue remains. The explicit and implicit bias resulting from that residue permeates every aspect of American society and affects almost every decision made in it, steadfastly working against the achievement of true equality.

---

10 Research has shown that, while the possibility of explicit bias does exist, implicit bias is far more prevalent in our workplaces today. See Dr. Arin N. Reeves, *Written in Black & White: Exploring Confirmation Bias in Racialized Perceptions of Writing Skills*, Yellow Paper Series (Nextion, 2014).

CHAPTER 2

The Continued Absence of Diversity

● ● ●

WHEN JACKIE ROBINSON JOINED THE Brooklyn Dodgers, major league baseball was shaken to its foundation. The big leagues were at last integrated. It was all anyone could talk about. Of course, the tally was one African American and 399 white guys, but nevertheless, integration had arrived. In today's parlance, some would say diversity had been achieved. And such is the current state of corporate America. There is minority representation, and people are keenly aware of this fact and some even have the audacity to celebrate as if real victory had been achieved. But that representation is the equivalent of 399 to one.

Diversity in corporate America is not quite a reality, certainly not in a qualitative sense. With the systematic closing of the doors of opportunity in the faces of young minorities, all in the name of equality, coupled with white male opposition to diversity programs,[11] white-male domi-

---

11   In a Harvard Business Review article, it was stated that "pro-diversity messages signaled to ... white men that they might be undervalued and discriminated against. These concerns interfered with their

nance with regard to key positions and the prevailing attitudes reflecting the underlying ingrained bias, both explicit and implicit, are not scheduled for fundamental change anytime soon. For example, in major corporate law firms over the last several decades, we have simply made no progress, at least not fundamentally.

Of the roughly fifty thousand partners[12] in America's major law firms, approximately 1.8 percent[13] are African

---

interview performance and caused their bodies to respond as if they were under threat. Importantly, diversity messages led to these effects regardless of these men's political ideology, attitudes toward minority groups, beliefs about the prevalence of discrimination against whites, or beliefs about the fairness of the world. This suggests just how widespread negative responses to diversity may be among white men: the responses exist even among those who endorse the tenets of diversity and inclusion." Tessa L. Dover, Brenda Major and Cheryl R. Kaiser, "Diversity Policies Rarely Make Companies Fairer, and They Feel Threatening to White Men," *Harvard Business Review*, January 4, 2016. Studies have shown that diversity policies can blind white men to racism and sexism at work and also lead to resentment and feelings that they are treated unfairly. See Justin Wm. Moyer, "Workplace Diversity Policies 'Don't Help' – and 'Make White Men Feel Threatened,'" *The Washington Post*, January 5, 2016.

12 National Association of Legal Placement, Inc. ("NALP") press release, February 17, 2015.

13 Deborah L. Rhode, Ernest W. McFarland Professor of Law, the director of the Center on the Legal Profession, and the director of the Program in Law and Social Entrepreneurship at Stanford University, wrote that in the United States, 88 percent of lawyers are white. She notes that "although blacks, Latinos, Asian Americans and Native Americans now constitute about a third of the population and a fifth of law school graduates, they make up fewer than 7 percent of law firm partners and 9 percent of general counsels of large corporations. In major law firms, only 3 percent of associates and less than 2 percent of partners are African Americans." Deborah L. Rhode, "Law Is the

American. And that percentage is inflated: many, if not most, African American partners are not equity partners. Many of the major law firms have both nonequity partners—partners who essentially are so in name only—as well as equity partners, those who have an equity stake and who are considered partners in the true sense of the word. Even those partnerships that are not officially tiered are tiered as a practical matter.[14] A disproportionate number of minority partners nationwide are not equity partners. At the end of the day, virtually nothing has changed since I started practicing law more than thirty years ago. Roughly 93 percent of the partners in the country's major law firms are white,[15] and 2.8 percent are Asian American.[16] Of the 4.2 percent sliver that is divided among African Americans, Latinos, and other trace-element minorities,

---

Least Diverse Profession in the Nation. And Lawyers Aren't Doing Enough to Change That," *Washington Post*, May 27, 2015. NALP notes in its January 2016 *Bulletin* that African Americans make up "not quite 1.8 percent of partners and counsel."

14 New figures from NALP show that in 2014 only 5.6 percent of equity partners were racial/ethnic minorities; "NALP Research: Despite Small Gains in the Representation of Women and Minorities among Equity Partners, Broad Disparities Remain," *NALP Bulletin*, June 2015. Equity partners in multitier law firms continue to be disproportionately white men; "NALP Research: The Representation of Women and Minorities among Equity Partners See Slow Growth, Broad Disparities Remain," *NALP Bulletin*, April 2014.

15 Rhode, "Law Is the Least Diverse Profession." According to NALP's November 19, 2015, press release, the number is 92.5 percent.

16 M. P. McQueen, "Minority Ranks at Large Firms Show Little Growth," *The American Lawyer*, May 28, 2015.

an even smaller number enjoy any real power and influence, because, as I stated, not all partners are created equal.

The boards of directors of major corporations and their senior management teams lag behind as well. In the Fortune 500 companies, more than 86 percent of directors are white.[17] The number for white representation is closer to 90 percent when it comes to these companies' executive management teams.[18] African American board representation is approximately 8.77 percent and trending down, while African American executive management representation is approximately 4.23 percent.[19] Of course, many companies have no African American or other minority representation on their boards or senior management teams, and for those who do, there is often overlap, since the same individual may serve on multiple boards.

In recent years, the ranks of junior associates and junior management have become increasingly representative in many instances relative to the numbers in the senior ranks, but retention and advancement continue to be an issue.[20] The hard, cold fact is that through the years, the

17 According to the study *Missing Pieces: Women and Minorities on Fortune 500 Boards* (2012 Alliance for Board Diversity), in 2012, 86.7 percent of Fortune 500 board seats were held by white men and women.
18 Senator Robert Menendez, *Corporate Diversity Report*, August 2010.
19 Ibid.

20 For example, see McQueen, "Minority Ranks": "More minorities leave law firms early than other groups, studies show. A 2010 study published by Nancy Levit and Douglas Linder of the University of Missouri-Kansas City found that half of lawyers of color leave law firms within three years, earlier than lawyers in general." And, "as has

face of power in corporate America has remained largely unchanged, and it would seem now that we are actually going in reverse.[21]

While an African American holding a position of power in corporate America is no longer cause for shock (or undue jubilation), since today there is some representation where yesterday there was none, African Americans are still largely absent. From my privileged seat as a senior

---

been the case since at least 2004, when we first broke out results by race and ethnicity, Asian or Asian-American attorneys were the best-represented minority group, with 6.4 percent of lawyers and 2.8 percent of partners. However, the large gap between the number of Asian partners and Asian nonpartners (9.3 percent) suggests they encounter obstacles to promotion." That said, the representation of African American associates has been declining every year since 2009—from 4.66 percent to 3.95 percent, according to "NALP Research: Women and Minorities at Law Firms by Race and Ethnicity—An Update," *NALP Bulletin*, February 14, 2014.

21 Gregory Wallace, in "Only 5 Black CEOs at 500 Biggest Companies," *CNN Money*, January 29, 2015, notes that there are only five African American CEOs in the country's largest companies. In other words, only one out of every one hundred Fortune 500 CEOs is African American. For all intents and purposes, that means that there aren't any, and the trend is not encouraging. Between 1999 and 2010, fourteen black CEOs were appointed at Fortune 500 companies. See Richard Zweigenhaft's article for Who Rules America, based on a presentation at the annual meeting of the American Sociological Association in New York City on August 12, 2013. The title of the article is as telling as it is chilling: "Diversity among CEOs and Directors: Has the Heyday Come and Gone?" Zweigenhaft writes, "The number of white women who were CEOs in each year since 2000 [through January 15, 2014] increased at a fairly dramatic rate...however, a new and unexpected pattern has emerged for the other underrepresented groups. By the end of 2013, diversity in the CEO position had declined for them."

partner in a major corporate law firm, I seldom see other minority faces around the conference table, in the board-rooms, or in the executive suites I frequent.[22] When I am sitting in meetings, I frequently take note of the racial makeup of the participants. It has become a game. At a board of directors meeting for one of my clients, sixteen people sat around the conference table: fifteen white men and me. No women. No other minorities. Contributing to a sense of isolation, it used to depress me. Then it made me angry. Now I just sigh and say to myself, "Really?"

---

22 Or, for that matter, in high-end hotels, high-end restaurants, first-class cabins, national corporate law conferences, etc., unless they are in subservient roles.

CHAPTER 3

We Mentor Those Who Look like Us

● ● ●

HARD WORK AND DETERMINATION ARE required for anyone to succeed in corporate America, but they alone are not enough. There must be an understanding of the game—an understanding that minorities are usually forced to discern on their own or not at all. They are too often left alone, peerless, powerless, and mentorless, navigating through shifting sands, fighting invisible forces, trying to hold on, playing a sometimes brutal game without knowing the rules, a game they are not expected to win. With the right mentor, they have a shot. Without one, losing the game is pretty much assured.

In corporate America, chances are good that if you are African American, those in the best positions to successfully mentor you will not seek you out. Often without thinking, people tend to gravitate toward and mentor those who look like them.

For the first several years of my legal career, I did not have a mentor—no one to guide and protect me, no one who knew me or cared to know me, no one committed to my success. As a result, I was placed on a path to certain failure, a path that I proceeded along blindly, while those in the know snickered in the background.

As a matter of substance, not much has changed over the years. Today, most organizations acknowledge the need for mentors and have accordingly established formal mentoring programs. The resulting relationships, however, are usually artificial and ineffective. They are little more than arranged marriages, and no bonding occurs. The assigned mentor goes through the motions and looks forward to the day when his charge may be discarded and his burden lifted.

For an African American just starting out, there is usually no one in a position of power who looks like him enough to be naturally attracted to serve as a mentor. The white men (they are usually white men) find themselves gravitating elsewhere. As a result, the African American is left to flail and fail. Of course, there are the rare exceptions. If there weren't, I wouldn't be here.

In many ways, for me, it all started with Alston J. Shakeshaft. When I was a freshman at Iowa State University, he was perhaps my first big break. He was a very special mentor and a very special man. First in his class at Yale and a veteran of D-Day and the Battle of the Bulge, this fiery political science professor was like my second father.

As an unsophisticated college kid, unaware of the ways of the world, I didn't understand the importance of a mentor, someone to guide me, to teach me the system, to show me the ropes and the traps, to champion my cause, and to impress upon me what I could do and should do.

I was brighter than almost everyone else, and I knew it from an early age. I eventually convinced myself that I knew everything, but, of course, relatively speaking, I knew nothing. I was poised to wander hopelessly off course in life, destined to ultimately tumble off a cliff to my academic death. But I didn't stray off course, at least not for long. I got lucky. Unsolicited, Professor Alston J. Shakeshaft stepped into my life as my second college advisor. My first college advisor had dropped me after just one quarter, dismissing me as someone with little promise. That proved to be my good fortune.

Because Shakeshaft entered my life, I pushed myself in ways I might not have otherwise. Because of Shakeshaft, I began to consider possibilities for myself I had never before imagined. Because of Shakeshaft, I went to Yale Law School, a rare and extraordinary opportunity enjoyed by a relative few.

At first, I couldn't figure him out. I couldn't decipher the gruff, unsmiling exterior. After our first encounter, I drew conclusions based on stereotypes of old white men, particularly old white men with perpetual scowls carved on their faces.

I dreaded my monthly visits to Shakeshaft's dimly lit, pipe-smoke-filled lair. There, trouble always lurked. Shakeshaft suffered no fools and had no tolerance for anything less than exceptional. During our discussions, he would browbeat me, seemingly mystified as to how anyone so stupid had been permitted on campus in the first place. I drew a conclusion. Clearly, this man was a racist. I could not have been more misguided about that.

It is true, Shakeshaft was never satisfied with me. My grades, my performance in class, were never good enough. He had gone to Yale. He was exceptional. I was something in the rough—either a diamond or a zircon, yet to be determined.

With eyes on fire, he would bellow through the smoke of his ever-present pipe. "Dammit, look at these grades! You do want to go to law school, don't you?"

"Well, yes," I would answer meekly.

"How in the hell do you expect to do that with this showing?" he would yell. I didn't think things were so bad. "You're not even trying!" But I was trying. I was trying very hard. "This is not good!" He continued on with his tirade. "You're coasting! Is that how you think you're going to get through life?"

"But I'm not coasting," I said, feebly attempting to defend myself.

"I don't know why I waste my time. God knows. For what?"

I swallowed hard.

"Now, please leave, and see if you can find it in you to be more productive. And stop parking your car wherever you damn well please! I think you have parked in every space on campus except the president's!" It seemed that, among other things, I had racked up around $300 in university parking violations, which was a lot of money for me at the time.

My grades weren't bad—all As and Bs. And the Bs usually had more to do with me getting in a professor's face about something rather than the merits of my performance. I once berated the economics professor teaching a class on the Western movement in the United States for lecturing on as if the West had simply been empty real estate waiting to be occupied, failing—indeed, refusing—to acknowledge the existence of Native Americans and the atrocities committed by European Americans in the name of progress and white destiny.

Few things are as heartbreaking as the stories of how we mistreated Native Americans. The crimes were monumental but largely ignored: the cruelty, the utter disrespect for their history, their culture, and their lives, all conveniently sanitized. All they did, all they had to offer, all they were made to endure…today, almost everyone agrees that Native Americans were wronged terribly, but I daresay, very few of us know the true magnitude of that wrong.[23]

---

23 While modern mass shootings are tragic, I have always taken issue with statements along the lines that such and such a shooting "is one of the worst massacres ever to occur in America." Today's mass murders generally pale by comparison to the mass murders of Native Americans—by the federal government, no less. Take, for perhaps the worst example, the Bear River Massacre in Idaho, a dawn raid by US soldiers on a winter village of the Northwest Band of Shoshone, resulting in the rape and murder of at least 250 (estimates run as high as 500) men, women, and children on January 29, 1863. The Native Americans'

Obviously, those of us born after the fact cannot be held responsible, but we should want to know the stories, and we do have an obligation to remember. Like it or not, this past is a part of who we are. But it is too often ignored or dismissed.

"There were people already here, you know. They were trying to live their lives in peace. They had families. They had hopes and dreams. They had a way of life. We took all of that. We destroyed it all. We stole their land. But that alone wasn't enough. We had to rape and murder them, too. We had to destroy their culture. We had to do all we could to erase them from the earth along with any evidence that they ever existed. We are no different than the Soviet Union and other regimes we have condemned throughout history for doing exactly the same things—throwing people out of their homes, pushing them off their land, committing mass murder. Violating women, killing children for sport. Why don't you acknowledge that? Why don't you talk about that? Why don't you talk about those who sacrificed everything to make all of this wonderful economic progress possible?"

The professor glared at me.

"Well?" I asked.

---

resources were very limited, and within thirty minutes, everything they had to fight with was gone. From then on, it was wholesale slaughter, with the soldiers shooting or bayoneting everyone they could find. See www.kuer.org/post/shoshone-mark-150-years-bear-river-massacre.

"This is an economics course," the professor replied. "If you want to learn about the Native American experience, you will have to go elsewhere."

"That's not an answer," I said. "You can't teach economic history and ignore the people who made progress possible or ignore those who were so profoundly affected. Shouldn't we be made to understand the ramifications of what we do? Shouldn't our choices be guided by their effect on others? On society? Without that understanding, I question the validity, and hence the value, of your course."

"You've made your point. May we continue now?"

"Continue what?" I asked. "Our discussion? I would be happy to."

"That is quite enough, Mr. Graham. In the future, please confine your remarks to what is relevant to this class."

"What could be more relevant?" I exclaimed.

The professor turned his back on me and proceeded with his lecture. I still got a B. But even with my sometimes impolitic behavior, I did very well overall. Very well, however, wasn't good enough for Shakeshaft.

It wouldn't be until much later that I realized that Shakeshaft was never satisfied because he knew I could always do better. Unlike those I would later encounter who were never satisfied because they refused to see my promise or to admit that I was every bit as good as my counterparts, Shakeshaft saw my potential and did everything in his power to make sure that it was realized.

One spectacular fall day as I was leaving my English history class, I received a note. Shakeshaft had summoned me. As I hustled across the sunlit campus, I tried to recall the transgression that must have been central to this particular summons, but I drew blanks. I had been on my best behavior, at least as far as I could remember. My grades were good. I no longer routinely parked illegally.

Arriving at Beardshear Hall, stately with its dome and towering columns, I hurried inside and ran up the grand staircase. Three flights later, I found myself outside Shakeshaft's office. I paused to catch my breath and gather my thoughts. Sweat poured from my forehead. I pulled out my handkerchief and wiped my face and neck, took a deep breath, and knocked softly. I waited a few seconds before trying the door. With some hesitation, I crossed the portal separating the normal from the paranormal. Instantly, the air quality plummeted. I peered through thick clouds of pipe smoke in search of my mentor. There he was, seated in the shadows, partially concealed by the stacks of books and papers cluttering his desk, his gruff exterior intact. I inched forward. No words were spoken. The only sound was that of Shakeshaft drawing air through his pipe. With each breath, sparks seemed to fly from it—and from his eyes.

"Come in! Come in!" he shouted, seemingly agitated as he waved a thick book in the air. Heart pounding, I sat down in a chair across from him. After more than two years, Shakeshaft still intimidated me, notwithstanding the fact that over time, I had seen the kindness of his soul slip through that tough facade, those times when he had inadvertently dropped his guard. I had come to understand the size of his heart and the depth of his generosity. But, yes, he still intimidated me.

Shakeshaft watched me, eyes bulging as clouds of smoke drifted toward the ceiling. He hadn't stopped scowling. As was his custom at the beginning of every visit, he looked me up and down, examining me, measuring me against some unarticulated standard in a vain attempt to ascertain any positive changes since our last meeting. He shrugged as if to say that the miraculous transformation for which he was waiting so patiently had yet to occur. He still couldn't figure out whether I was a chrysalis or a maggot. That made us even; I couldn't figure him out, either. I sat still, trying to breathe, palms sweating.

At last, Shakeshaft broke the silence. "Listen to this!" he roared. He gathered himself and began to read some vague language out of the book, repeatedly poking the page with his index finger for emphasis. I listened. He read some high-sounding words about the need for the legal profession and law schools to become more diverse and provide greater opportunities for minorities. "Do you know what this means?" he exclaimed, gesturing with his hands, puffing madly on his pipe. He was so excited, he could hardly contain himself.

I could not share in the excitement, however, because I had no idea what he was talking about. As near as I could tell, Shakeshaft had finally gone mad. He had snapped.

Moreover, breathing through all the smoke was becoming increasingly difficult. My brain was oxygen starved, and my eyes were stinging. Shakeshaft, however, was oblivious to the surrounding pollution. He was too excited. He was excited for me, something I would not fully appreciate until years later. He was excited because, beneath that tough, worn exterior, he cared deeply about his students. He cared deeply about me. He could not have loved me more had I been his son. He had made a thrilling discovery that would have a tremendous impact on my future, and he couldn't wait to tell me. For the moment, however, I was befuddled. I squirmed in my chair, pretending not to be bothered by all the smoke.

"Don't you know what this means?" Shakeshaft nearly shouted. I made barely audible sounds and shifted my weight. "This means that you can go to any damn law school you want to!" He slammed the book onto his desk. I flinched. I eyed him and tried to sort out the meaning of the interview. "Harvard, Yale, Princeton!" Shakeshaft exclaimed, reopening the book and thumbing through its pages. He was like a freight train already out of control yet still gathering momentum. He was on a roll. "Princeton would be great for you. Yes, Princeton." He thought for a moment, flipping pages. "No. Princeton would be perfect, but it doesn't have a law school."

He flipped through more pages, reading with lightning speed, puffing madly on his pipe, lowering the oxygen level in the room to the point where human life could no longer be sustained. "Yale, though…that's a thought," he mused. His eyes slowly rolled toward the ceiling. "Yes. Why not Yale?"

I was in the room, but Shakeshaft was having a conversation with himself. The near-incoherent babbling was making no sense to me. Suddenly, he shifted the focus of his energy from the book to me. He locked onto my eyes with such ferocious intensity that I lost what little breath I had remaining. Unsmiling, he issued his final challenge. "I'm not sure if you are smart enough," he said. He paused for effect. "You have to show me by turning in a couple of four-oh quarters. Do that, and then I will back you. I will get you into Yale."

I sat there as my mind left my body. The whole scene, from start to finish, was unreal. My mind was spinning from the smoke and the heady mention of faraway, exotic places.

Harvard. Yale. These words were not in my vocabulary. Oh, yes, I had heard about such places, as I had heard about London and Paris, Venus and Mars. But I had never thought of going there. It was not that I ever intentionally excluded myself—it was just that places like Harvard and Yale were not a part of my world, and no one had ever told me that they should be. Other kids might have grown up to see Harvard and Yale as options, if not entitlements, but not me. As a child, expectations for me were not defined in terms of an Ivy League education. A white man who, initially, barely knew me changed all of that. A white man with the courage to insert himself into the life of an African American kid changed all of that. It didn't matter to him that I didn't look like him, and it certainly didn't matter to me. What mattered to me was having a powerful mentor by my side. I could have cared less about his color. What mattered to him was my life.

I went on to get close enough to the 4.0s, and Shakeshaft wrote six or seven letters of recommendation. The last few he wrote grudgingly. "This is a damn waste of my time," he would say. "You're going to get into every law school you apply to. You should stop wasting my time and yours." As always, Shakeshaft was right. I was admitted to every one.

Those were exciting times, collecting all of those acceptance letters. Without Shakeshaft, however, it never would have happened, because I never would have tried. I wouldn't have known to try. I would have survived, but without Shakeshaft, I might not have thrived.

Without my mentors, primarily Alston J. Shakeshaft in college and Tom A. Alberg when I was a young lawyer, who knows what would have happened to me? It's one of those what-ifs that we can't answer, because it didn't happen. What I can say is that without these two white men taking a sincere and active interest in my future, I doubt that I would have gone to Yale, and I doubt whether I would have made partner at Perkins Coie.

Nothing good can come out of not having a strong mentor. Among other things, every organization has a system, a way of doing things, a way of measuring achievement. Without a mentor, the system can never be learned, not completely, and full integration can never be achieved. It's tantamount to moving to a foreign country and never learning the language or the culture. You'll never be integrated and will never achieve citizenship. No one ever mistakes you for a native. Instead, everyone smiles and is nice to you as they wait for you to leave.

Too many African Americans in corporate America today mistake the smiles for something sincere, failing to appreciate that those polite, seemingly interested individuals, those who promise opportunity but seldom follow through, are just waiting for them to leave.

CHAPTER 4

Blacks Need Not Apply

● ● ●

WHEN IT WAS MY TIME to leave home and head off to Yale, I stuffed my maroon 1965 Mustang 2+2 with all my important belongings, together with my memories of growing up in Ames, Iowa. It seemed like I had been in that benign, white bubble for decades, but it had been only thirteen years.

What I would miss most about Ames was my father. The Iowa State University campus had been our common battleground for the preceding four years, me the political science major, he the engineering professor. Our paths would often cross as we rushed in and out of buildings from class to class—Dad walking purposefully in a sport coat that didn't fit, looking anything but resplendent in a clashing discount-store shirt and tie, not a natural fiber in sight,[24] a man on a mission, focused inward. He would

---

24 Sartorial splendor was something that would never come to mind regarding my father, but he always dressed nicely. Foremost for him was not looking good but self-defense. He believed that it was much safer being a black man in America if you were wearing a coat and tie.

be off in some other world, heaven knows where, but he would see me and stop in his tracks. His weary face would light up with pride at the sight of his second son. He would peer through his glasses with tired eyes and ask me how I was doing and where I was going. After some good-natured kidding, we would say our good-byes, and he would march off in his worn Hush Puppies.[25] I would look after him fondly, wishing that I could do more to bring joy into his life. Always thinking, *Someday*, never stopping to realize that the joy brought to him by my mere existence was immeasurable.

Nearly every day, I would walk past the old Victorian building housing my father's cramped second-floor office that he shared with a colleague. If his well-worn,

---

25 My father, Frederick Mitchell Graham, PhD, was a professor who taught engineering mechanics (the ins and outs of stresses, strains, and vibrations in structures) to would-be civil engineers. He was extremely bright. He supported himself during his early college days by working all night in the packing house, sleeping and studying on the bus and saving the daylight hours for classroom work. World War II saved him from working himself to death, and after returning home from the South Pacific, he was able to complete his education under the GI Bill. Graduating at the top of his class at Iowa State with his master's degree in 1949 and having served his country well in the army, he sought a job in industry. No one would hire him. He saw white students who had not performed as well as he had readily find good jobs. Every door in industry my father knocked on, however, remained closed. So he took the job that was available to him, a professorship at the historically black college Prairie View A&M. He never made it into industry. He also never complained. The only reason I know anything at all about these experiences is that his sisters told me. They were heartbroken, and I daresay bitter, over the treatment received by their little brother when he tried to enter corporate America.

black three-speed bicycle was chained to the rack there, I would know that he was on campus somewhere, and I would yell up to the window. If he was there, he would stop grading papers or preparing for class or talking with a student, or whatever he was doing, and look out through the screen. He would see me and yell down. I would call him "ugly man" or something like that, and he would call me a "so-and-so,"[26] and then I would be on my way.

Sometimes instead of yelling, I would just walk up to his office to see if he was in. I would sit in his desk chair, shake my head at the equations on the chalkboard, use his phone, share his sack lunch. All of that was now coming to an end. I wouldn't be stopping by anymore. I was moving on.

I drove nonstop from Ames to New Haven with the help of my older brother. Less than twenty-four hours after leaving Iowa, we rumbled to a stop at 127 Wall Street, New Haven, Connecticut, the site of the imposing Gothic complex that is the Yale University School of Law.

Peering out from the Mustang, I surveyed my new surroundings. I was overwhelmed by the magnificent architecture and intimidated by three hundred years of history. It was hot, it was humid, and I was tired to the point of hallucinating. I studied the gargoyles perched high above on stone ledges and shrank under their gaze. I felt the weight rising on my shoulders from the knowledge that I would soon confront the brilliance of the faculty as a frightened first-year law student, a 1L from central Iowa, a bit player

26 My father never swore. The closest he ever came was "Dadgummit."

on a stage that had been occupied by past and future US Supreme Court justices, lions of industry, future US presidents, and a whole raft of others well out of my league.

Yale had seemed like a good idea in the abstract, but now that I was on campus, I had second thoughts. The number-one law school in the world—what was I doing there? As my first few days as a Yale student passed, breathing the rarefied air didn't become any easier, and my anxiety grew. I perceived my classmates as too smart, too well read, and too well traveled. Compared to them, I concluded, I was little more than a country bumpkin. And it didn't help to hear comments from white students such as, "When I completed my application, I wrote on the back of my picture, 'No, I'm not black.'" Or, "What are you worried about? They would never flunk out a black guy." I had entered a new and unfriendly world, or at least one with a hard racial edge that I wasn't used to. I had stepped out of my Iowa bubble and was about to discover the true meaning of racism.

I had showed up at Yale completely clueless about many things, including the major corporate law firm world. I had no idea how big law firms worked, what it took to succeed in them, the nature of their practices, the internal politics—none. I did understand, however, that the major corporate law firms were where the wealth and power of the legal profession was concentrated. So I'd blindly applied for entry into that world. For my efforts, I was promptly slapped down and kicked to the curb. Unfortunately, I did not understand that African Americans, for all practical purposes, were not welcome.

A common misconception held by the general public (and by quite a few law students) is that law school teaches one how to practice law. It does not. A finishing school for newly minted lawyers is required. There are many of these; major corporate law firms can fill such a role. Typically, to land a position at one of these firms, a student must first spend the late summer and fall of her second year interviewing to be a summer associate between law-school years two and three. If she succeeds and her luck continues, she will be offered a job and will spend the following summer at the law firm. She then will attend law school for one more year, graduate, and return to her firm to begin practicing. Every fall, the dance begins anew as, in a continuous wave, firm after firm arrives on campus to interview a select number of would-be lawyers.

When I participated in this dance, many of the interviewers had no interest in even seeing a black law student, let alone inviting one back to their firms—something I had to learn the hard way.

In one case a partner from a Chicago firm confided that his firm was not ready for a black lawyer. An older gentleman, he said that he didn't agree with his colleagues, but that was the reality, so he knew that he would not be doing me any favors by bringing me in the door. He was unwilling to play the game so often engaged in by large firms today of hiring African Americans with no honest intention of ever seeing them make partner. He told me sadly that I would have to find my opportunity elsewhere and wished me luck. He was polite and respectful. During the interview, we had talked about Yale, law, life, and the state of the world. Later, he wrote me a letter concluding with the following bit of advice: "Don't let the bastards get you down."

Soon thereafter, I confronted a Chicago law firm partner cut from a different cloth. My interview had been scheduled for one of the guest suites just off the law school courtyard. I entered the dimly lit room, extended my hand, and introduced myself. Although we exchanged pleasantries easily enough, her haughty expression belied her true feelings. She spent little energy on concealing her contempt. Others who allowed their prejudice to quickly guide them to a negative conclusion about me had at least engaged in small talk and feigned interest between glances at their watches, but not this woman. My feelings were not to be spared. My rejection had to be total, my annihilation complete. The massive assault began immediately. I didn't stand a chance.

Her first question was something on the order of why I thought I belonged at Yale. Innocent enough—until the next question. "Do you honestly think that you are qualified?" Naïve and unsuspecting, I had walked into a mugging. The slap was unexpected and caught me completely by surprise. My heart accelerated, and my head spun. She moved in for a quick kill. "Isn't it true that you are at Yale only because of affirmative action?"

My face went blank. What kind of question was this? I tried to gather my wits. "I suppose that it depends on how you define affirmative action," I responded. "In some ways, everyone here is here because of affirmative action. Because of their connections. Because of who they know."

"Don't be clever," said the woman. "You know what I mean." I had never been in an interview like this one. I was unprepared. I tried desperately to get my bearings. On a roll, she stormed on. "Come on, you're taking someone else's spot. Do you honestly think that you are qualified?" I absorbed another slap in the face. "Why are you interested in working at a major corporate law firm, anyway?" she demanded.

My throat went dry, and I had difficulty moving my tongue as I tried to answer her questions calmly and evenly, not taking issue with their legitimacy.

She added, "Most blacks go to work for the government. Wouldn't you be more comfortable in a government job?"

I felt that I was being called a nigger over and over by someone in a position of authority, but I sat there in my cheap suit with my sweaty palms and took it. I took it because I thought I had to take it, and I didn't know what else to do. This was foreign territory for me. I was being pummeled verbally by someone who could influence my future. I was being demeaned and disrespected, but I had no power to fight back; at least I believed myself to be powerless. It was me against the world.

I began to feel sick. What had triggered this onslaught? Why was this particular interviewer so vindictive, so hateful? In her mind, so it seemed, I didn't belong at Yale, and she was going to prove it. She was condescending, insulting, dismissive, and patronizing. Her questions, her tone of voice, and her demeanor sent the clear message that she was a big-shot Chicago law firm partner, and I was an insignificant African American devoid of promise, imposing on her precious time. I had thought that America had moved beyond that sort of direct assault and that, at least in terms of corporate racism, more subtle approaches were in vogue. I was wrong.

I wanted to scream at her, I wanted to break a lamp over her head. But those were not practical options, so I sat there, frozen by history and by personal experience. I was still trying to get a job, trying to gain entry into a world that I knew little about. I had no handbook and no one to guide me.

Eventually, I recovered from the surprise attack and regained my footing. I stopped the interview. I wasn't sure what was going on, but I knew that to continue would be pointless. "You know," I said, suddenly past caring, "I really don't think that I have to take this from you or anyone." I was done. If this woman was playing by the rules, then I was getting out of the game. "This is bullshit," I told her. "I don't know a lot. I am not as sophisticated as you. Maybe I'm not even as smart as you. But I do know that this is bullshit. Your feelings are obvious. Your beliefs are obvious, and they are incompatible with mine. It is clear that you have no interest in me but only contempt. There is no need to continue wasting each other's time."

I stood up to leave, no more than ten minutes into a thirty-minute interview. The partner was stunned. Her mouth opened, but this time, no words came. I guess she wasn't used to people walking out in the middle of her performances. I picked up my resume and left the room. The partner panicked. "Wait! Don't go!" she shouted. I am sure the urgency in her voice surprised even her.

"I have had enough," I called over my shoulder. "I really can't stand any more." I walked out, leaving the partner looking bewildered and unsure.

As I headed along the stone pathway, down a few steps and into the courtyard, the interviewer gave chase, calling out, but I didn't turn around. I just kept walking. There was a slight chill in the air, though it was effectively warmer than the temperature in the interview room. I felt momentary triumph. I had called bullshit on a big-city partner and walked out. I felt powerful. I also felt angry. If anyone had crossed me at that moment, I might have punched them, giving credence to the stereotype.

I heard the partner's footsteps on the flagstones behind me. "Wait!" she shouted.

I didn't stop.

She picked up the pace and grabbed me from behind. I stopped and turned around. I looked at her but said nothing. We stood in silence for a moment. She spoke first. "I meant no offense," she said without conviction.

I frowned. "You're kidding, right?" I said. "I don't know how you could have been any more offensive. And now you're standing here, expecting me to believe that you meant no offense?" I started to turn away.

"No! Wait! Okay. I was wrong. I made a mistake."

I just looked at her. I was at a loss. The whole incident was surreal. She had gone too far. We both knew that. It was time to try to clean up this mess.

"Okay," she said. "I'm sorry. I apologize."

Suddenly, it would seem, the tables had turned, giving me the leverage. I had no interest, however, in striking back or otherwise trying to get even. "Apology accepted," I said without feeling.

It is doubtful that the partner was truly sorry. She indeed might have been surprised by her own insensitivity or her own recklessness. Perhaps she was all at once fearful of lawsuits or a reprimand from her partners or from Yale. I was still interested only in getting a job.

We completed the interview in the courtyard. She asked me the questions she should have asked at the beginning. We wrapped things up and said our good-byes. A few days later, she invited me to Chicago for a full set of interviews—just for cover, I suspect. I flew to Chicago, however, and met with her colleagues. Her firm seemed inclined to extend me an offer and asked that I not make any decision until I heard back from them. I had seen enough, though. I accepted employment elsewhere.

CHAPTER 5

The Isolation Chamber

● ● ●

WHEN I GRADUATED FROM YALE Law School in 1976, I joined the largest law firm in Seattle—Perkins, Coie, Stone, Olsen & Williams—as its first black attorney. I can recall only one other black employee. The total number of African American lawyers at Seattle's three or four largest firms at the time, including me, was about four. Seven years later, I became the firm's first African American partner, joining three other African American partners in the largest firms in Seattle. I had successfully navigated a river so treacherous that I wonder if I would even have tried if I had known or appreciated at the beginning what I knew, and certainly appreciated, at the end.

Most of my tenure at Perkins, which lasted until 2000, was as the firm's only black attorney. I left to start the Seattle office of Orrick, a global law firm headquartered in San Francisco.[27] Today, I am extremely fortunate to find myself

---

27 I owe a tremendous debt of gratitude to the partners at Orrick, led by Mark Levie, Ralph Baxter, and Lee Jay, who, with open minds and enviable courage, recruited me, built an office in Seattle around me,

at Fenwick & West, certainly one of the leading technology
and life science law firms in the country, if not the world.[28]
I will be forever grateful to our former chairman, Gordy
Davidson, whose vision and determination in recruiting me
and opening a Seattle office gave birth to the opportunity.
My partners have, for the most part, been good partners to
me and I am quite fond of many of them. It is a cohesive group
I am honored to be a part of. The support I have received
over the years has been extraordinary, and the firm has been
generous and fair. That said, we have approximately 115
partners, but only two are African American. Accordingly, if
I were to leave, the number of African American partners at
the firm would decrease by 50 percent. To state the obvious,
if only two partners left the firm, and they happened to be
us, the number of African American partners would drop to
zero.

The firm has been in existence for over forty years. It
boasts a solid culture grounded in mutual respect, collabo-
ration, and hard work. In terms of diversity, its collective
heart seemingly is in the right place, but its progress has been

---

and ultimately made me the head of the firm's corporate group world-
wide. After eight years, the marriage fell apart, as marriages sometimes do, but I will always look affectionately on those years and be
appreciative of the opportunities that resulted.

28 At the time of this writing, Fenwick & West LLP listed among
its numerous significant clients Cisco, Fitbit, Uber, Apple, Google,
Facebook, Twitter, Symantec, and GoPro. Average annual compensation for its partners exceeds $1.5 million.

limited[29], in significant part due to its lack of self-awareness and its eagerness to applaud incremental steps and bold talk while avoiding fundamental change.[30] This state of affairs is more or less replicated across corporate America.

While there is much talk among leaders of organizations about improving diversity in the upper echelons of their businesses, the results of this are unimpressive.[31] Although many of these leaders are quick to speak in righ-

---

29 This is not an exclusive club – hundreds of millions of dollars have been spent across corporate America on diversity programs over the years with little effect. See, e.g., Shankar Vedantam, "Most Diversity Training Ineffective, Study Finds," *Washington Post*, January 20, 2008; Peter Bregman, "Diversity Training Doesn't Work," *Harvard Business Review*, March 12, 2012.

30 For example, at an executive committee meeting, one of my partners was exalting the firm's progress in the area of diversity and announced that among other, similar firms, ours led in every category. I expressed disbelief and asked, "Even African American partners?" My question provoked knowing laughter, since I was the firm's only African American partner at the time. One partner said, "Well, I am sure that we are leading among Silicon Valley firms in the category of African American partners based in Seattle who are at least six feet four inches in height." As of early 2016, the firm had ten African American attorneys, eight of whom joined in or after 2011. Between late 2008 and early 2016, nine African American attorneys left the firm.

31 Deborah Rhode noted that "the problem is not lack of concern. I recently surveyed managing partners of the 100 largest law firms and general counsel of Fortune 500 companies. Virtually all of the 53 participants in the study said diversity was a high priority. But they attributed the under-representation of minorities to the lack of candidates in the pool...such explanations capture only a partial truth. Minorities' under-representation in law school does not explain their disproportionate attrition in law firms." Rhode, "Law Is the Least Diverse Profession."

teous generalities, the actual numbers are both dismal and seldom articulated. It is as if by not talking about the numbers and simply declaring that they stand for what is right, it is easier for leaders to ignore that the status quo continues, and they don't worry too much about the absence of change.

By avoiding focus on the numbers, it is easier to project an illusion of progress. By declaring a crowd diverse after sighting a single black face, it is easy to lose any sense of urgency, particularly since diversity, for many, is not really a top priority, anyway. We cite as progress the fact that there are five CEOs of Fortune 500 companies who are African American, patting ourselves on the back while conveniently avoiding focus on the fact that there are 495 who are not. Indeed, including the current five, there have only been fifteen African American CEOs in the history of the Fortune 500.[32] To the surprise of no one who is paying attention, we stagnate as a society, failing to acknowledge that we will see little improvement as long as we argue that change is not urgent or even necessary.

Although most leaders in corporate America are quick to condemn blatant bias in the larger society, they tend to turn a blind eye to the subtle strains of bias pulsing within their own organizations, doing little to counter their effects. Focused firmly on profit generation, they are unconcerned if opportunity is not allocated fairly, failing to fully appreciate how all bias, the seemingly insignificant

32 Ellen McGirt, "Why Race and Culture Matter in the C-Suite," *Fortune*, January 22, 2016.

transgressions within their own organizations and the more egregious behavior in the larger society, is connected and symbiotic, all contributing to the creation of an environment conducive to racism.

I would expect nothing more from any high-flying corporation dominated by white men gravitating toward other white men in terms of forming associations. Much of this is the result of conscious decision, though I would like to believe that the larger part is the result of unconscious bias. Many have little or no appreciation for how their action or inaction promotes and solidifies systemic exclusion and undermines the status and careers of women and minorities.

As a law firm associate, I was required to fight my battles pretty much alone. It was a world of isolation and exclusion. Among my colleagues, I had no one to talk to who looked like me, no one who truly understood. A number of times, I made the mistake of trying to make others understand, but too often, at the mere suggestion of bias, I was deemed a hypersensitive malcontent, seized by paranoia and mentally trapped in a bygone era characterized by pervasive racism, a world that bore no resemblance to modern society—or so it was explained to me. Mention the possibility of racism, and the partners became rigid and defensive, issuing strong denials with a lot of throat clearing and howling at the ridiculousness of the mere thought that anyone at the firm could possibly be biased on any level. This pretending continues on today: the status quo is preserved. If we say we are not biased enough times, then we must not be.

After I made partner at Perkins, I found myself one night sitting at a table in a private room of an upscale restaurant with thirteen other partners. We were at an elaborate farewell dinner for a partner who had decided to leave the firm to join a client. Wine flowed as I listened to our departing partner recount some of her experiences over the years, describing battles she had fought as a woman breaking into the firm and into the profession. It hadn't been easy, she said, but she had made it. Critical to her success was the comfort and essential support provided by other women lawyers as they had helped her to shoulder the burden. It had made the struggle bearable and the difficult much less difficult. It had given her strength and made success possible.

The other women there nodded in agreement, recalling how at each transgression by their male colleagues, they would huddle in the women's restroom to dissect the event and plot strategy. I just listened and thought of my own battles during the same period with no one by my side. I'd been wounded repeatedly by stinging insults and insensitive affronts but without a support group to commiserate with me and share the deep feelings of frustration.

The isolation continues to this day, and I find the lack of diversity progress in corporate America a source of profound disappointment. Virtually all of my colleagues and clients are white.[33] As if this weren't enough, I continue to operate pretty much alone in terms of sustaining and expanding my practice.[34] That approach is fine and it served me well in terms of developing a power base and independence, but a little extra wind under my wings in the form of institutional opportunities would have made me feel more like a member of the club.

As a law firm partner, I have seldom been asked by another to accompany him or her on an important pitch or had a significant opportunity referred to me internally.[35] I can, however, think of any number of times when I was either ignored or nudged aside even though one could argue that I was an obvious choice. And of course there were those significant opportunities that were mentioned once

---

33 Of course, I have nothing against white people. Half my family is white. I do, however, have something against the absence of African Americans.

34 While all law firm partners other than so-called service partners are expected to be self-sustaining, there are those "self-sustaining" partners who reap significant benefit from institutional opportunities (opportunities essentially generated by the institution), opportunities that I have been all but excluded from over the years.

35 Deborah Rhode notes that "substantial evidence suggests that unconscious bias and exclusion from informal networks of support and client development remain common. Minorities still lack the presumption of competence granted to white male counterparts." She goes on to add that "women and minorities are often left out of the networks of mentoring and sponsorship that are critical to career development. In American Bar Association research, 62 percent of women of color and 60 percent of white women, but only 4 percent of white men, felt excluded from formal and informal networking opportunities." Rhode, "Law Is the Least Diverse Profession."

and never again. Throughout my career, there has always been a justification or rationale for not including me, expressly excluding me, or otherwise not encouraging action that would expand my business base or network. When others were pitching work, putting together brochures, describing the partners in our group, discussing adding partners highly relevant to my position, responding to external inquiries, or passing down relationships, I often became invisible. I assume the negative actions of many of my colleagues over the years had less to do with naked bias and more to do with external forces, real and imagined, coupled with the failure to stand up to those forces.

I remember the night I found a stack of pitchbooks sitting at the front desk, ready for a meeting the next day with a prospective client. Casually checking to see if there was anything new in our approach to marketing, I picked up a copy and thumbed through it. To my surprise, the book included the bio of every partner in my group except me.

Once, a partner from another firm stopped me on the street and informed me that during a deposition, one of my partners had been asked to name all the partners in my group. He had listed every one except me. Similarly, I learned from an accountant that when a group of my partners were pitching him for referral work, one of them claimed to represent one of my clients. The accountant responded by saying, "I thought Steve Graham represented them." My partner replied, "Oh, yes, but I consult." It was a lie. He had no relationship with my client.

Another time, one of my partners invited every partner in my group to a business-development affair—that is, every partner except me. The lone nonwhite partner in the group was excluded (and, by the way, a white senior associate, a nonpartner, did receive an invitation). I wondered if the partner had actually thought to exclude me. I assumed that it was even worse—I just didn't register. I did not exist. I was invisible. When this individual pictured his colleagues, they were all white. I confronted the partner, and he apologized. He said he was sorry for not thinking of me. I did not question his sincerity. Like so many, he simply didn't understand the nature of his own bias. But, whether he was sorry or not, the effect on my career was the same; I had been excluded and thus denied an opportunity afforded every other partner in my group (and one nonpartner).

In a world virtually devoid of African Americans, behavior that encourages our systemic exclusion and that promotes and intensifies feelings of isolation is our daily bread. As a result, we limit our participation in the organization's activities, feeling less than enthusiastic about joining in with a group indifferent to our presence. This only adds to the speed at which the isolation gap expands, eventually leading to our departure and leaving others in the organization to scratch their heads in wonder at why African Americans don't seem to want to stay.

CHAPTER 6

"Go to Hell, Nigger!"

● ● ●

I WAS STANDING ON A playground in central Iowa as an eleven-year-old, trying to fit in as the only nonwhite kid in my class—or, for that matter, in the entire school, other than my little sister. My crime, other than being born black, was misjudging a fly ball and letting it fall to the ground in the middle of a softball game. My classmate was furious with me. I tried to explain that I was trying and hadn't intended to screw things up. He responded by yelling at me, "Go to hell, nigger!" I remember that incident particularly well because he said the statement with such feeling, such hate, and such utter condemnation. The son of a prominent doctor, perhaps he was just repeating what he had learned at home. Whoever the teacher, he had learned his lesson well.

With those four words, I suddenly stood naked on the playground, stripped of all dignity, revealed as something subhuman and deserving only of contempt. Laid bare was the lie I had lived every day, the lie that I was just like everyone else. On that day, fantasy collided with reality, and my world blew up. It would have hurt less if the boy had whacked me with a baseball bat. Much less. Such can be the power of words. Shattered and reduced to tears, I ran back inside the schoolhouse and into the arms of my sixth grade teacher, Mrs. Hadden. She tried to comfort me, but she didn't understand. How could she? She was white.

No one has yelled "Go to hell, nigger!" in my face lately, but I have been called a nigger nonetheless, many times, as I stood alone, the only African American in the room. While people tend to be more subtle these days, the sentiment remains clear. Certainly, the *N* word is not used, and sometimes no words are used at all. Much of the communication is nonverbal, with those giving it often failing to appreciate what they are communicating. But make no mistake about it: I am reduced to something inferior and of no consequence. And while the *N* word may not be used, at least to my face, at times—in even professional settings—people have come painfully close, using words like "darkie" or "mongrel," or issuing a death threat, or just calling me an asshole, or otherwise treating me with open disdain by, for example, ripping documents out of my hand or slamming my office door. And sometimes it is just a whisper emanating from behind a polite façade.

Early one morning, I found a large group of people assembling in our Seattle conference rooms. I asked the Bay Area partner overseeing the proceedings what was going on. He smirked and said, "I can't tell you." At first, I thought he was kidding, but he wasn't. He wouldn't tell me anything. Somehow, he had come to the conclusion that he couldn't trust a senior partner who was head of the Seattle office to maintain a client confidence regarding a major meeting taking place—in the Seattle office. I shook my head in disgust and walked away. Shortly thereafter, I learned what the transaction was all about—from an associate.

CHAPTER 7

Stacked Deck

● ● ●

IF YOU ARE AFRICAN AMERICAN, you start out in corporate America with at least one strike against you, sometimes three. It is hard to get to first base under those conditions and nearly impossible to reach home. For skeptics, I note the recent study showing that law firm partners graded identical legal memos differently depending upon whether they believed the author to be white or black.[36] While the study is new, the reflected racism is not.

Navigating corporate America is not easy for anyone, but for women and minorities, there is always something

---

36 In the study, a legal memo was given to law-firm partners for a "writing analysis." Half the partners were told that the author was African American; the other half were told that the author was white. Other than race, the memo and the "author's" name and record were exactly the same. The partners gave the memo they believed to have been written by a white man a rating of 4.1 on a scale of 5, while the memo believed to be written by an African American received a rating of 3.2. The "white man" received praise for his potential and analytical skills; the "African American" was said to be average at best and in need of "lots of work." Overall, the "white" memo was evaluated as better in regard to analysis of facts and had substantively fewer critical comments. Reeves, *Written in Black & White.*

extra to overcome. Always. It can be tantamount to stepping over a puddle (a mere annoyance) or staring into an abyss the size of the Grand Canyon, depending on the day and the task and the protagonist, but there will always be something extra creating friction and headwind, working steadfastly to slowly erode an otherwise promising career.

The typical experience for the African American associate in a major law firm, or anywhere in corporate America, is to have no old-boy network to tap, no allies outside the firm, and only modest referrals from within, if any. She is pretty much on her own as she fights against the headwinds of racism, striving to achieve success in a world long closed to, and still foreign to, persons of color.

In the law firm context and across corporate America, an African American is viewed through a different lens, and information about her will be processed differently, a reflection of the broader society. Once, I was alone on the elevator in a parking garage. I stood in the back, left-side corner. The elevator stopped, and a white man got on. He went to the back-right corner. At the next stop, a white woman got on. She entered from the left, so she didn't see me; she was looking at the white man and smiling, though they clearly were strangers to each other. Then she noticed me. The smile instantly evaporated, replaced by a frown. I was a successful law firm partner, but to her, I was a big, scary black man. I smiled in an attempt to put her at ease, something I spend too much time doing (smiling in an attempt to put white people at ease). Why is it that black people often mistake me for a medical doctor, while too many white people dismiss me as a thug?

Just a few months ago, I was in a restaurant, waiting for my takeout order. A white woman was sitting on a stool nearby, waiting for the rest of her party to show. When her friends arrived, she got up, leaving her purse hanging on the stool. I took a few steps toward her and said, "Excuse me." She recoiled and looked at me as if to ask, "What the fuck do you want?" I directed her to her purse. She seemed confused as she tried in vain to convert her distain to gratitude.

Throughout my tenure at my first law firm, I was continually accused of trying to intimidate, for no apparent reason other than the fact that I was a big, tall, smart black man in a position of authority who demanded perfection. To this day, I remain a big, tall, smart black man in a position of authority who demands perfection. For some, that is terrifying. Early on, I often failed to appreciate that, as an African American, thanks to the subliminal messages swirling about and perpetuating age-old stereotypes, too often I would be deemed unfit or unworthy of promotion or retention, or indeed even feared, as the result of characteristics that are routinely overlooked or even applauded when possessed by a member of the majority.

An aggressive white associate is applauded as a tough negotiator, while an aggressive black associate is condemned as hostile and antisocial. A witty white associate has a good sense of humor, while a witty black associate is deemed not serious. A caustic white associate is clever, while a caustic black associate is mean, someone people won't know how to deal with. An unflappable white associate is cool under fire, while the unflappable black associate is seen as being uninterested, disengaged, and not excited by the practice. If an African American fails to smile all of the time, he is deemed angry or intimidating. If an African American questions an assignment, he is deemed insubordinate or unwilling to do the work. If an African American questions the way he is treated, he is deemed thin skinned, paranoid, and difficult to manage. If an African American is forceful in his convictions, he is deemed a bully. If an African American is relaxed, he is deemed not to care.

A messy office is ignored, or it becomes an endearing trait, if the associate is white. If the associate is black, it becomes a problem and is accepted as evidence of a disorganized mind. If a white associate wears clownish socks, he is deemed lighthearted and fun. Such attire worn by a black associate is taken as proof positive that he is not to be taken seriously. If you are white, your outstanding performance is applauded. If you are black, it is deemed the result of affirmative action or luck.[37] If you are white, your divergent opinion is deemed a different point of view. If you are black, it is deemed to be wrong.

---

37 As an example, once I literally single-handedly saved an initial public offering at the eleventh hour. I was a hero to the lead investment bank, and the accounting firm partner bowed in my presence. My deft handling of the circumstances was quickly forgotten, however, and never led to any additional work.

CHAPTER 8

Modern Racism and Compromised Principles

● ● ●

WE USED TO BE ABLE to readily identify the opposition. Not so much anymore. Racism has morphed, although sometimes I fear that overt racism in making a comeback.

In many ways, and perhaps fundamentally, American society is unchanged from the Jim Crow days. We would like to believe otherwise, what with the coming of Barack, the appearance of a black CEO at a non–African American corporation here and there, the occasional sighting of a black partner in a major corporate law firm. But let's not kid ourselves. Racism in polite society hasn't disappeared; it has adapted. It has mutated. There are times when the racist blows his cover, inadvertently failing to use the code, and we are allowed to see the danger. But the disguise is quickly re-applied, the smile returns, and we are left to wonder whether our eyes and ears have deceived us. We are lulled into thinking that since racism is less loud, it must be less prevalent.

Too often, it is the illusion of progress we see. Unfortunately, that illusion is often used to justify doing nothing more to correct the undercurrent of bias and the resulting imbalance. It is at these times that the ink becomes visible, as successful African Americans are celebrated and offered up as evidence that all is well.

Helping to create the illusion and ensure that racism stays strong are those who compromise their own principles because they lack the courage to counter the bias of those they seek not to offend. They extend the hand of acceptance and opportunity to minorities, only to quietly withdraw it, without explanation, when someone of influence expresses disapproval. I am reminded of a time when my kids were small. My wife served them dinner, and my son, who was three or four at the time, turned to his big sister and asked, "Do we like this, Aimee?" Too many members of the majority are willing to challenge bias only if it seems like the popular thing to do. Only if it is convenient. Only if someone of sufficiently high stature says it's okay.

Personally, what I find most distasteful is the dishonesty, more so than the actual bias. People should have the spine to admit their own bias, or at least acknowledge the effects of bias practiced by others, instead of allowing stereotypes to be played out and giving support to the narrative that minorities just don't measure up.[38] I have

---

38 Of course, there are those who do not own up to their bias simply because they are truly unaware of it. Speaking of awareness, once one of my white partners, in trying to describe to me how busy he was, retold part of a story. He couldn't remember the name of the story, so he asked me if I could. I told him that I could not. Actually, I could, but

experienced transparency at this level only once in my career—when that partner in the Chicago law firm said he was in favor of hiring me but that his partners would not accept me. No excuses—just the unvarnished truth that his partners were not interested in hiring a black man.

Of course, that sort of transparency these days would be met with a lawsuit. So we continue to go in circles. Those prone to bias are left with no choice other than to continue to denigrate African Americans to give legitimacy to their actions. And those less inclined to openly denigrate do so with their inaction—for example, by promising to assist but failing to follow through. Or promising to include African Americans when new opportunities are presented, but failing to do so. Instead of the welcoming sounds of inclusion, African Americans are too often met with silence and empty promises. The presumption of incompetence, or less competence, made by the partner, the contact, the potential client, serving as the basis for the silent rejection, is left unsaid. No explanations are given as African Americans are left to ponder in isolation.

---

this particular partner was such a nice guy I didn't have the heart to tell that he was describing a scene out of *Little Black Sambo*. I know he would have been horrified if I had.

CHAPTER 9

Legitimizing Rejection

● ● ●

MOST WHITE MEN AND WOMEN in positions of power in corporate America have never interacted with an African American as an equal but only as someone less educated or subordinate. Even fewer have experienced an African American supervisor. Under these circumstances, especially when all the racial baggage is taken into account, it should come as no surprise that they think of white colleagues and other white individuals first when assigning work or choosing someone to take along to pitch new business, or visualizing someone as their partner or as their lawyer, or otherwise accepting someone as their equal. Notwithstanding good intentions on an intellectual level, society has taught many of us to instinctively react negatively to certain cues. That initial negative reaction carries over and colors much of what happens next. Many earnest individuals who would never consciously make a decision based on race have acted, and continue to act, on their ingrained biases, thereby subconsciously denying opportunity.

There are those, however, who believe (or who want to believe) that African Americans do not have what it takes on the merits. They hesitate to say it too loudly (usually), but they believe, or want to believe, that African Americans come up short intellectually. They work hard to move the goalposts if need be to prevent or erase African American accomplishment or to ensure that the accomplishment is simply ignored.

I have faced this phenomenon any number of times, beginning in college. It seems that some take it upon themselves to begin early the process of preserving the status quo through suppressing African American accomplishment. If an African American does not receive credit earned along the way, he eventually can be rejected and kept in his place on purely "objective" grounds. In other words, later evaluators are able to point to lower grades or less experience and reject on those merits, so all is fair and as it should be. But if the lower grades aren't there, they just make stuff up.

This sleight of hand continues throughout the years as reality is bent to conform to underlying racism, ultimately resulting in immeasurable economic damage to the African American community, a fact underappreciated by the larger community. This unbiased bias is exemplified by studies such as the one I mentioned where law firm partners graded identical papers differently depending on whether they believed the author to be white or black.[39]

---

39 A form of this "unbiased bias" was noted in Reeves, *Written in Black & White*. The law firm partners who were more critical of a memo they believed to have been written by an African American tended to show bias when collecting data but not when assessing that data, thus preserving the myth that they were, in fact, unbiased: "The

In anticipation of attending law school, I took a constitutional law class in college. It was one of the more difficult political science courses, taught by one of the more difficult professors. I was the only African American in the classroom of aspiring would-be lawyers. The balance of the thirty or so students was white. On the first two tests, I had the highest grades in the class. In fact, one other student and I did so much better than everyone else that the curve became distorted, forcing grades on our classmates much lower than they otherwise would have received. For the final exam, the professor told the two of us to take the day off to give the others in the class a chance at a more reasonable grading curve.

Notwithstanding the fact that I was an African American, the professor was willing to accept, and indeed celebrate, the fact that I had performed at a level higher than the balance of the class. There were other professors, however, who were cut from a different cloth. For

---

data findings...illustrated that the confirmation bias on the part of the evaluators occurred in the data collection phase of their evaluation processes—the identification of errors—and not the final analysis phase. When expecting to find fewer errors, we find fewer errors. When expecting to find more errors, we find more errors. That is unconscious confirmation bias. Our evaluators unconsciously found more of the errors in the 'African American' [associate's] memo, but the final rating process was a conscious and unbiased analysis based on the number of errors found. When partners say that they are evaluating assignments without bias, they are probably right in believing that there is no bias in the assessment of errors found; however, if there is bias in the finding of the errors, even a fair final analysis cannot, and will not, result in a fair result."

one, though I performed at the highest level possible in his class, he could not accept it, so he rewrote the rules. Or was he simply warning me of the unwritten rules?

Usually, when people launch baseless attacks on others, they try to be subtle about it. If unable to conceal their action altogether, they attempt to at least manufacture some seemingly legitimate support for their position. In college, my international law professor saw no need for such formalities. He decided to shoot me in cold blood, in broad daylight, in the middle of Main Street. I had earned an A in his course, but he didn't want me to have an A, so he gave me a B. All of his tests were multiple choice, and I had scored an A on each one, having answered all the questions correctly. There was nothing subjective. Still, I was given a B. I asked why.

"Because you weren't trying hard enough," he said. He seemed angry that I found his exams so easy. Or perhaps he was angry because we both knew by then that my options for law school had been narrowed to Harvard and Yale. Maybe, though, in his own misguided way, he was trying to do me a favor.

"But I did everything that I needed to do to get an A," I replied.

"Maybe so, but it is time that you learned how to try harder. You didn't work hard enough in my class." He was going to teach me to work harder by denying me what I had earned? Giving the professor the benefit of the doubt, however, perhaps he was trying to signal me, trying to sound the wake-up call that in our world, an African

American cannot expect to succeed without being twice as good and doing twice as much as the white person sitting next to him. Moreover, he should get used to the idea of not receiving what he has earned.

"Hey, listen," I said. "I did what I had to do."

"And not an ounce more!" replied the professor. Was he warning me that, for African Americans, being as good is not good enough?

"Then make your tests more difficult!" I said.

"That will be enough," said the professor as he turned to walk away.

I stared at the back of his head, speechless, not knowing what to do—not sure if I had even fully understood the encounter. I started to follow him, but after a few steps, I stopped. I shook my head and let it go. I didn't need the grade; grades no longer mattered. I had already been admitted to every law school I had applied to.

In any case, the incident caused me to ponder my position and what lay ahead in my life. If this was how it was going to be when the tests were objective, what chance did I have with the subjective? What chance did I have if the literacy test was always going to be changed on the day of the election? I was concerned, but I was too naïve to understand how concerned I should have been. Looming ahead was an attempt at a law firm career. What I didn't know was that it would be difficult to find a series of tests more subjective than the challenges confronting an African American associate venturing to advance through the fraternity of a major corporate law firm—perhaps not as difficult as it was for a black man to vote in Mississippi in 1950, but the same idea: accomplishment and what was right could not be expected to carry the day. Remember, again, that recent grading study.

A few years before my encounter with my international law professor, when grades did matter, Joanne, my future wife, and I took a course together and ended up collaborating on our papers. We helped each other with editing and rewrites. Joanne is white. The completed papers were similar in all material respects, but the professor deemed them otherwise. In time, our grades were announced, and Joanne received an A, while I received a B.

In my mind, there was no reason that the grades should have differed. I approached the professor and asked for an explanation. He politely explained to me that my work just didn't quite measure up. Joanne had received a higher grade because, in the professor's opinion, her paper was much better written. I enlightened the professor about the history of the papers and how they related to each other, but he was unmoved. I politely but strongly insisted that he show me a material difference between them. He seemed taken aback by the strength of my arguments and my resolve. In many ways, he seemed to be seeing me for the first time. He hesitated, no longer so sure of himself.

"Don't waste your time," I said. "I can tell you right now that you can't. You may try, but you will not. There is no material difference."

Having no specific response but unwilling to back down, the professor attempted to manufacture arguments for why Joanne's paper was superior, but he only achieved incoherency. As I had warned, it was not possible to articulate any meaningful difference between the papers other than the races of the authors. Persistent, if nothing else, the professor continued stumbling and stammering in a feeble attempt to justify his predetermined conclusions. In the end, he surrendered. There was no substance to his arguments, and he had to admit it. He changed my grade to an A.

There is no way of knowing the number of times over the years that similar circumstances have occurred without redress.[40] The black man doesn't do as well simply because he is assumed to be incapable of doing as well. He is judged in a different light. His work receives a biased review and a resulting discount. He may do just as well as the next person, or better, but somehow, when viewed through the lens of racism, his performance just doesn't quite measure up.

So the first punch typically received by African Americans in the workplace is courtesy of those who believe the African Americans' work to be per se inferior even if equal to or better than the work product of their white counterparts. The second punch comes from the unfair allocation of opportunity, the cumulative effect of which is to lay the groundwork to legitimize future

---

40 Indeed, if I had worked on my paper in isolation and received a B, it is unlikely that I ever would have challenged the grade.

negative evaluations and ultimate rejection. When, after several years, the black employee is compared to the white employee, the white employee comes out on top on the merits. The black employee is given projects and opportunities sporadically and never allowed to build momentum or develop an expertise, as limited opportunities result in limited experience. With limited experience, the African American employee is not chosen for the next project, because he is not as accomplished as the more experienced white employee. Accordingly, the white employee is presented with the new opportunity. Over the years, the gap widens, one small step at a time, as the cycle works to slowly erode the career of the African American employee. Eventually, reality catches up to the initial bogus negative impression, and the self-fulfilling prophesy is realized.

I have seen partners react with sincerely puzzled looks when I have questioned whether they have truly provided a minority associate with a legitimate opportunity. If an individual is to learn and advance, she must be given a series of repetitions strung closely together so that real experience can be had and real expertise developed. Otherwise, after a few years, those in power can say, honestly and without a hint of bias, that the individual who has been denied opportunity is not qualified, failing to see the unfairness in their "honest" assessment.

And by "repetitions," I do not mean the opportunity to watch someone else perform a task multiple times. I do not mean several chances given to someone that are separated by months, resulting in "opportunities" so few and far between that it becomes nearly impossible to actually build any momentum or expertise. "Repetitions" does not mean scolding someone and quickly pushing her aside to allow "someone who knows what they are doing" to handle it when in the early going she doesn't get something quite right or proves not to be fluent, instead of showing support and offering encouragement, making it clear that you have her back. If an organization is serious about training, it must allow for failure followed immediately by a chance to do better.

In other words, an individual must be given a true opportunity to learn. If opportunities are not sustained, each rare opportunity is tantamount to starting all over, so the associate doesn't improve. As a result, she is unfairly deemed to be not as skilled or, worse, incompetent. (It is no different from the days when blacks were prevented from learning to read and write and then condemned as stupid for being unable to read and write.) Her opportunities then become even more limited as her incompetence or skills deficiency is considered confirmed, and the organization begins to write her off. It is the difference between assuming someone has the potential and encouraging her and giving her the opportunities to learn and to practice and to get it right versus assuming that someone has little potential and essentially dismissing her from the start, casting her off, going through the motions, and providing no real opportunity for her to develop the skills needed for success—and then condemning her for lacking those very skills. It is the difference that results from the fact that minorities still lack the presumption of competence granted to their white male counterparts.[41]

---

41 Rhode, "Law Is the Least Diverse Profession."

CHAPTER 10

Nurturing Bias

● ● ●

IT IS THE RARE WHITE person in a position of influence in America who has never heard an arguably racist remark during a whites-only conversation. I myself don't believe that such a person exists. I'm not talking about someone using the *N* word—that would be too obvious. I am talking about all the damning little side comments relating to competence, affirmative action, attitude, and the like that nourish the seeds of doubt. It is also rare for these influential individuals to take issue with such remarks, judging by what I have seen personally. If they won't take issue when an African American is present, I can only imagine the behavior when everyone in the room is white. Indeed, there are those who actually join in, reaffirming the "appropriateness" of the remarks, even if only said in "jest." No need to take a stand, particularly if it may lead to someone's discomfort. Just chuckle, join in, or simply stand by silently, giving your tacit approval, whether or not that was your intent.

A major reason that negative attitudes persist is the fact that too often, when we hear an offhand remark, we let it go. It is almost as if to say that as long as a particular minority doesn't hear the slur, it is okay. No one is hurt as long as no one hears. Besides, taking issue involves risks. We find comfort and safety in pretending that things are much better than they are, and given the thin veneer of civility firmly in place most of the time, we tend to get away with our pretending, successfully keeping reality at arm's length.

One day at Perkins Coie, I was standing in my office with an associate. We overheard one of the secretaries talking to two other associates in the office next door. They were discussing the attributes of yet another associate. The secretary said, "I thought that the only way to get a job here with those kinds of credentials was if you were a minority hire." The racist sentiment was clear.

The three of them shared a chuckle, all in good fun, perpetuating the idea that minorities, even at a law firm the caliber of Perkins, were somehow less qualified and hired on the basis of something other than merit. I turned to the associate standing in my office and said, "I think we just heard a racist remark."

He said, "I think we did."

Afterward, I spoke to both of the lawyers who had participated in the little murder. The associates were decent young men, but they were both white, and it was clear that they both had little appreciation for the consequences of their inaction. Alone in their offices, one-on-one, I explained to them that in my view, the remark denigrating the abilities and qualifications of the firm's minority lawyers was inappropriate and that I hoped, after consideration, they would share my view. I explained to them that the cumulative effect of the repeated utterance and acceptance of such seemingly innocent remarks was the perpetuation of the myths and the prejudice and the negative presumptions so damaging to minorities. I told them that I expected more in the way of leadership from them. If they truly disapproved of the remark, which I had found insulting, they should have voiced their disapproval. Unless they believed that the minority lawyers at Perkins were less qualified and less capable than the white lawyers, they should have used this as a "teachable moment," an opportunity to mentor the secretary, instead of standing by and allowing the remark to go unchecked, thereby enabling the roots of bias to inch deeper.

Each of the associates said that they understood. (What else could they say?) They said that they believed the remark was wrong and that they were wrong to respond in a way that suggested agreement. I accepted them at their word. They assured me that they did not share the view expressed. They had done nothing to stop the spread of racist sentiment in this instance, however, because they hadn't wanted to make the secretary feel uneasy. Is it any wonder that prejudice continues? We don't want to make others feel uneasy. We don't want to feel uneasy ourselves.

Even when I am present for a remark like this, the result can be the same. Once, I found myself at a firm dinner, engaged in conversation with the partner sitting across from me. Two or three seats down, one of our colleagues made a racially insensitive remark. I heard it; I am pretty sure the partner sitting across from me heard it, judging by the subtle change in expression. But amid all the chatter, it was easy to pretend otherwise. There was a split second as he waited for my reaction. I chose to ignore the remark so as not to draw attention to myself. He, too, said nothing, but I am sure for different reasons. Showing leadership and courage in such moments can be difficult.

While I was a partner at Perkins, an African American associate brought to my attention a racially insensitive project being led by two of my partners. I, in turn, brought the project to the attention to one of the senior partners. He moved decisively and had the work removed from the firm. One of the many interesting aspects of this particular incident was the way in which the two partners, I believe cluelessly, engaged in this behavior that essentially disrespected their African American colleagues. They then proceeded to double down on the disrespect by arguing that the firm should check with the NAACP to determine whether their African American colleagues were right to be offended. When I later asked the managing partner to take action to insure against the recurrence of such behavior and to take steps to make it clear that the firm supported its minority personnel, he told me that he was fully supportive and would back me up on anything I did. That was nice, but I would have preferred that he take the lead.

There will be little change until the vast majority of those empowered to make change consider change a priority; until a significant number of those empowered to make change take the initiative instead of standing on the sidelines, waiting to support the initiatives of others; until those in leadership positions stop with their tepid, canned "celebrations of diversity" and instead forcefully acknowledge bias and move aggressively to do something about it, to hell with the risks.[42] If you are not working to end bias, then you are working to preserve it.

---

42 The following words of Martin Luther King, Jr. are instructive in the context of bias and ineffective diversity programs in corporate America – "I have almost reached the regrettable conclusion that the Negro's great stumbling block in the stride toward freedom is ... the white moderate who is more devoted to 'order' than to justice; who constantly says 'I agree with you in the goal you seek, but I can't agree with your methods of direct action;' who paternalistically feels he can set the timetable for another man's freedom; who lives by the myth of time and who constantly advises the Negro to wait until a 'more convenient season.' Shallow understanding from people of goodwill is more frustrating than absolute misunderstanding from people of ill will. Lukewarm acceptance is much more bewildering than outright rejection." *Letter from Birmingham Jail.*

CHAPTER 11

Corporate Chattel

● ● ●

Mark Twain offered the following recipe for success: just combine ignorance with confidence. Although I never heard that advice when I was coming along, that is precisely how I approached my legal career. I had plenty of confidence, but I had no idea of what I was getting into with major corporate law firms. If I had known, there is a good chance I would have looked elsewhere for a career. Largely due to my upbringing, I never focused on the near-complete absence of minorities and women in any position, let alone positions of power, in corporate America.[43] In this

_____

43 I spent the first eight years of my life in Prairie View, an unincorporated, all-black town in East Texas. During this period, issues having to do with race were largely abstract for us because, day to day, we never interacted with or even saw white people. When we stepped out of our secure enclave and ventured to Houston or Galveston or some of the smaller white towns near Prairie View, we were subjected to the usual indignities of the Jim Crow South, but these were not part of our daily life (although I do recall my mother defiantly lifting me up to use the "white" drinking fountain in a Houston department store). When I was eight, we moved to an all-white town in the Midwest: Ames, Iowa. On more than one occasion growing up, I experienced the bitter taste of racism, but I never attributed unpleasant incidents to a particular

environment, I struggled to reach first base. And after I managed to succeed in spite of it all, there were those who continued to work to limit my success to the fullest extent possible.

Many African Americans entering corporate America are unaware that their chances of ultimate success are much lower than they imagine. Few hints are given, because diversity is on everyone's lips and political correctness is on everyone's mind. Not that much has changed since I first stepped into this world so many years ago, a world where my opportunities would be diverted, achievements discounted, and opinions unheeded until articulated by someone of a lighter shade. I arrived brimming with confidence and excitement, oblivious to harsh reality. I had drawn the role of the clueless black kid from small-town Middle America, having no experience whatsoever with corporate America—the kid who, more by chance than by design, had landed on the doorstep of that all-white bastion of Republican males, Perkins, Coie, Stone, Olsen & Williams, whose partners were keepers of a system that had inoculated the firm against African Americans in ways not even they were any longer aware of.

On that first day, I stood in the elevator lobby in my cheap, double-knit suit and fat polyester tie, newly minted Yale Law degree tucked under my arm (with a translation of the Latin stuck to the back). I walked into a twilight

---

race, only to particular individuals; this was largely because every friend I had, and every nurturing adult outside of my home, was white.

zone of broad smiles and curious stares. It was as if I were a talking dog—a black associate in a major corporate law firm, the first black lawyer Perkins had ever hired in its history of seventy-some years. Indeed, I can recall only one other black employee—Brian, in the mailroom. I had arrived to the consternation of more than a few, to the delight of many, to the surprise of all. I had little idea of what I had really gotten myself into.

I did not appreciate the difficulties I would face, the near impossibility of achieving my goal of making partner. Gender and ethnic diversity were virtually nonexistent in this world into which I had blindly sought admission and was now about to seek success. I assumed that the playing field would be level. It would not be. I assumed that the rules would be explained, that I would be given the same chances as everyone else. It didn't happen that way.

It wasn't long before I began to feel like the experiment I apparently was—there were the second-rate assignments, and the racist comments flowing from the mouths of a couple of drunken wives of partners at summer outings, betraying true feelings of some and causing me to wonder and fear how deep the expressed sentiment ran. Even many of the well-meaning had trouble getting past the negative presumptions that had been reinforced throughout their lives, often calling me not by my name but by the name of some other black person they had met.[44] I began to wonder

---

44 Even after I had made partner, one of my colleagues once approached me thinking I was the black summer associate and invited

why I had been hired in the first place. It seemed that half the partners were convinced that I could not succeed, and the other half feared that I might.

My supervising partners did not trust me with significant work or with significant relationships. My tasks revolved around research memos, reorganizing files, delivering checks, and the like. I was something of a Yale-educated file clerk doing busywork, seldom brought along to meetings and never allowed to participate in a meaningful way.[45] When I asked about it, I would be reprimanded for complaining. My expression of concern would be, in the eyes of my detractors, twisted into an unwillingness to do junior-associate work. Very early, some began to build the case that I was a malcontent, difficult to get along with, unwilling to pay my dues, abusive to the staff. These criticisms were fabrications, but I have no doubt that many of the partners sincerely believed them. After all, they fit the stereotype and served to confirm the underlying bias.

In fairness, in the big-law-firm environment, anyone's talent can be overlooked, and one can easily win an

---

me to accompany him on a trip to court so I could see what it was like. I needed no greater proof that too many in my firm and in the business world often looked at me without seeing me.

45 One supervising partner saw me as useful to bring along on lunches with his secretary to help disguise the affair that they were having. In response to what proved to be the final invitation, I exclaimed without thinking, "Again?" I fell into complete disfavor after that, and no more invitations ensued. I became, literally, good for nothing.

undeserved reputation as the result of one incident or of rumor. In the high-performance world of a major corporate law firm focused on providing the best in client service at any personal sacrifice, practiced at squeezing entirely too much work into the accelerated time frames demanded by clients, it's hard on everyone, and there are many casualties. But it's a great deal easier to disappear in the resulting rapids if you happen to be an African American associate. There is equality in that every associate is asked to ford a deep and swift stream in the dark with no sleep, but only the black associates are asked to do so with two-hundred-pound packs on their backs. Every young associate must read and analyze reams of complex documents, but only the black associate is required do so with a gun to his head.

You already know that I had no natural mentors, no power or support network to engage. No one else's success was at all tied to mine. Moreover, without a mentor, I didn't know what it was I was trying to do. In a word, I was flying blind. I had yet to fully appreciate that every organization has a system, a way of doing things, a way of measuring achievement. I didn't know the system. I didn't even know enough to know I didn't know.

No one coming out of law school has the knowledge needed to succeed at a major corporate law firm, so every associate begins in a fairly precarious position with much left to chance. But a black associate has added to this the pressure of having to constantly overcome the negative presumptions built into the system. Her energy is sapped by the continued drain caused by having to prove and re-prove herself, the need to do more, and to do it better, than her white counterpart. One mistake for the white associate and it's apt to be, "Okay, she had a bad day." One mistake for the black associate and it's, "Well, what did I tell you?" The white associate is presumed competent and judged as an individual. The black associate is presumed incompetent and prejudged in accordance with the still-prevalent stereotypes as a member of the racial minority long held in the lowest esteem by the white majority, the only racial minority defined by the least among them. Over the years, the texture changes, the strategies evolve, the code is refined, the racism becomes increasingly subtle, but fundamentally, the story remains the same.

In hindsight, it seems that many of the partners were just playing along, saying the right things, and waiting for me to leave of my own accord. Little did I know, but there existed a group who had no intention of ever supporting my entry into the partnership. My wife was told by another partner more than once, "They will never make Steve a partner." Can you imagine how that made her feel? As for those partners, the strongest encouragement they ever gave me was to leave the firm.[46] Their moves were similar

---

46 I was often told by certain partners how much better my life would be outside the firm, in a less challenging environment. Those at small firms were held up as examples of attorneys who enjoyed the good life, able to take time off to go watch the kids play baseball whenever they were so inclined, and the like. These partners in effect left a revolver on my desk and invited me to blow my brains out. I didn't accept the invitation.

to those of congressional Republicans who met at the time of Barack Obama's first inauguration to plot strategy to ensure his failure.

If I had been willing to blend into the woodwork, take what was given, and allow others to define my role and my career path, everything would have been fine, more or less. I did the opposite. I worked to define my own role. I resisted being slotted into a niche convenient and comfortable to others. I was outspoken and demanding. As a result, I was labeled an ingrate and difficult.

I tried to close my mind to the racism and usually succeeded, but on some days, I stumbled. Some days, mental fatigue overtook me, and my defenses collapsed. The burden of being alone, under attack, and unable to express my views for fear of being misunderstood—and continually being misunderstood anyway—took its toll. I had no one to talk with or vent to who truly understood. I had to do my best to deal with colleagues who couldn't quite figure out how to deal with me, who failed to realize that simply treating me the way they treated everyone else would have been a good start. Indeed, that tenet is all any organization in search of an effective diversity policy needs to follow.

I wondered at times if some of them even realized how different their greetings to me were compared to their greetings to their white colleagues. One set was dished out cold and professional, the other warm and embracing. I barely appreciated the difference myself until the day when they happened almost simultaneously. Side by side, as a partner who had recently returned from vacation greeted first me and then one of our colleagues standing in the hall nearby, the contrast was remarkable. It was as if I didn't belong. And, I suppose, I didn't.

Although I was with these people every day, many never saw me. I was invisible. Many of those who never saw me were in power and in control of my future. These were the individuals who would call me John or Jim or some other name that wasn't mine.[47] I would speak to them, but too often, they chose not to hear me. Caught in a void, I was someone to usually dismiss, someone to never fully embrace. Many times, I had colleagues bump into me in the office late at night, and I could read the fear in their eyes until they realized that the large black man in their presence was me.

Many of those deciding my future assumed that I was incompetent and held fast to that belief even in the face of evidence to the contrary. When I did something well, my detractors would shake their heads in disbelief or frustration, troubled by the facts. They would keep wondering why and how, perhaps attributing it to luck, never stopping to think that maybe I was pretty good.[48] Year in and year

---

47 Absurdly enough, a partner once called me by the wrong name and actually got upset at me for correcting him!

48 During the period when I did a fair amount of commercial finance work, I developed an expertise in ship mortgages. I then helped another associate get up to speed on the subject matter. Later, I had cause to ask a partner a question about ship mortgages. He directed me to the associate whom I had trained, describing him to me as the expert in the office.

out, my successes were brushed aside as the partners continued to predict ultimate failure, having already written my last chapter. I lamented about this fact one day with one of my Jewish friends. He said, "Yes, I know how you feel. Everybody assumes I'm smart just because I am Jewish. It puts so much pressure on me!" That comment, for me, confirmed the existence of parallel universes.

One morning, I found myself in the corner office of the senior partner to whom I had been assigned—we'll call him Hudson. Essentially, I was his indentured servant. We sat, reviewing the letter I had written seeking an attorney general opinion favorable to our client. For me, it was another exercise in discouragement. My so-called mentor, the man tasked by the firm to guide this stage of my career, never showed any interest in helping me to succeed. Instead, he wanted to prove that I could not. It was fixed in Hudson's mind that it was not possible for me to excel or to perform above a certain predetermined low level. As a result, when I did excel, Hudson viewed it as a fluke, never wavering and holding fast to the notion that I would never be as good as the other associates. Simply put, he had deemed me inferior and incapable of a strong performance. No fact to the contrary would change his mind.[49]

---

49 I place Hudson in that category of persons who view themselves as not racist because, for instance, they truly do not dislike African Americans. They are not hateful, but they still view black people as inferior and naturally unqualified for certain positions—in my case, partnership in a major law firm. Their thinking is in the same vein as Theodore Roosevelt's, who, while creating quite a stir by inviting

Hudson constantly rode me. Day in and day out, there was never a word of encouragement. At best, there would be damning with faint praise. He would refuse to give me work and then ask me why I wasn't busy.[50] "You can tell the successful associates around here. They are the ones who are busy," he would say, leaving it to me to figure out the rest. Once, he got on an elevator already occupied by me and another associate. In an attempt at humor, I asked him if he had gotten off on the wrong floor. He ignored me but acknowledged the other associate.

There were days when his attacks, overtly hostile or wickedly subtle, depending on his mood, would literally make me physically ill. There were the put-downs, the belittling remarks, the naked disrespect, the marginalization. Quitting, of course, was not in my DNA. I had no intention of voluntarily leaving the firm, at least not until

---

Booker T. Washington to the White House for dinner, nonetheless was of the view that blacks were a "perfectly stupid race." *American Ideals* (New York: G.P. Putnam, 1920), 279.

50 At one point, instead of providing me work, the firm "loaned" me to the United Way campaign. I became a "loaned executive" and essentially worked full time on the campaign, focusing on engineering and architecture firms, groups that had not been particularly responsive to the campaign in the past. One associate remarked that I was being treated like chattel, something he would never tolerate. Although I was on loan, I was nonetheless questioned by partners about why my hours were down. I am sure the exercise did not go as planned by some, because I did an excellent job in leading my portion of the campaign and in the process raised my profile and reputation in the community, helping to build a public reputation at odds with the narrative hawked by my detractors.

I had learned as much as possible about the practice of law. It was welcome to throw me out, but I wasn't going to quit. Moreover, I was smarter than most and, in my opinion, that included Hudson. I was determined to prove it despite the political consequences. My attitude, so it seemed, only served to give Hudson more resolve to see to my destruction.

Hudson would give me drafts of letters and memos that he had prepared and ask me to proofread them. By the time I returned them to him, they bled with red ink. I wondered after a while why he played this game.

One day, feeling particularly vindictive, I ripped into one of Hudson's letters. In the margins, I had written comments such as "This makes no sense! What is this supposed to mean? Completely incomprehensible. Awkward," and "Where did you learn to write?" After I finished venting, I could not very well present my provocative markup to my boss, so I retyped the letter, incorporating my revisions and throwing away his draft. I then walked down the hall to Hudson's office and placed the redraft on his desk. Shortly thereafter, he darkened my door. I looked up from my desk. He held the redraft in his hand. He wasn't smiling. "What did you think?" I asked.

No answer. Hudson stood before me in silence, red-faced.

I tried again. "Did you like the redraft?" I inquired. Silence.

Finally, unable to contain himself any longer, he erupted. "Where is my original draft?"

I froze. This development was unexpected. Production of the original draft would mean certain death. I fought the natural inclination to glance at my wastebasket. "I don't know?" I weakly responded.

"What do you mean, 'I don't know?'" Hudson snarled.

"I guess I threw it away," I said. Another stupid response.

Hudson's red face grew redder. "Geez!" he said, voice dripping with the customary contempt. "That was my work product!"

I was surprised by the reaction. What was this "work product" stuff? And why was he so proud of it?

"You had no business throwing away my work product!" he sputtered. He proceeded to lecture me on my misbehavior, pounding another nail into my coffin.

I tried to will Hudson out of my office before he discovered the markup in my wastebasket, lurking and ready to explode in my face. "I will see if I can find it," I said with my heart in my throat.

Hudson glared at me and stepped back. Not another word was spoken. He turned and disappeared.

I jumped up from my desk and closed my door. I fished the crumpled piece of paper out of the wastebasket and smoothed it out as best I could. Feverishly, I worked to make the offending remarks go away by writing over them and then scribbling over the new writing. I then hustled down the hall to deliver the cherished "work product" to Hudson.

In any case, back to the day when we were in Hudson's office, reviewing my draft letter to the attorney general.

He was busy finding fault with everything. He was convinced, or at least he was still trying to convince himself, that I could not write. He should have picked something where his bias would have been less obvious. For years, middle-school and high-school teachers and then Yale professors had praised my writing ability, sometimes describing it as poetry. One could say many things about me, but that I had an inability to write was not one of them. Still, Hudson knew the conclusion he wanted to draw, and nothing was going to stop him. Any contrary facts were to be dismissed as misleading. He was entitled to his opinion, after all, and in his opinion, I could not write. He trudged ahead, taking apart my work, nitpicking, moving from the subjective to the more secure ground of the objective, or so he thought. He zeroed in and focused on my alleged pathetic misuse of one word.

"And another thing: your use of the word 'inscrutable.' Why did you describe the law as inscrutable? How can a law be incapable of corruption?"

I smiled. *Here we go again*, I thought. "You got me there," I replied. "I have no idea how a law can be incapable of corruption. For now, though, it would seem that you don't know the definition of inscrutable."

"What?" Hudson frowned. A hint of uncertainty flashed across his face, quickly suppressed.

"Incapable of corruption. That's not what it means. It means 'impossible to figure out.'" I sighed.

"No, it doesn't," Hudson snapped, dismissing me out of hand. It had become reflex.

"Are you serious? When you don't know something, do you just make stuff up?" I asked in a misplaced attempt at humor. "Well, I'm afraid that you are wrong, but don't take my word for it. Go look it up."

Hudson's jaw tightened. No words were uttered.

I coolly eyed him.

Hudson continued to sit motionless, staring at me.

"You do have a dictionary, don't you?" I gently asked.

"I am certain that I am right," blurted Hudson, tight-lipped and sitting still, showing a firm reluctance to seek independent confirmation.

"Well, I am certain that you're not," I said. "Go look it up," I urged. "Let's see who's right. Let's end the suspense."

Finally, Hudson rose from his chair, muttering under his breath, and made his way to the other side of his office. He shot a glance at me. If looks could kill, I would have been dead.

Yanking his dictionary from the bookcase, he cracked it open, almost ripping it in two. He flipped madly through its pages. He stopped flipping and nervously ran his finger down a page, murmuring "inscrutable" over and over.

I smiled, crossed my legs, and assumed a relaxed position.

Hudson found the word. He read the definition and frowned. His pale complexion grew paler. He stared at the offending page in disbelief. He blinked hard several times in a vain attempt to bend reality to his will. Reality didn't budge. He slammed the book shut, unable to hide his disgust. His face screamed anger and embarrassment. Now knowing what I already knew, he literally stumbled back to the table, a little less erect in his bearing. He tripped on the way back and almost fell, catching himself and avoiding further embarrassment.

"Who are you so mad at?" I asked, almost sadly. "Me or yourself?"

Hudson just glared at me.

Once again, he had swung at me and had missed badly, throwing himself off balance. Once again, he had allowed his deep-seated bias to lead him astray. It seemed as if he would never learn. No one was winning this little game.

Hudson sat down and said nothing. I waited for his next move. An apology would have been appropriate, but I knew that none would be forthcoming. "I will get back to you with any additional comments," Hudson said, waving his hand to signal that I had been dismissed.

Hudson tried never to say anything good about me. He acted like it hurt to say anything positive. Once, when we were sitting with a client, a letter I had drafted in response to a German company's demand came up. Hudson tried to brush it off, but the client jumped in with unbridled enthusiasm, exclaiming, "Oh, yes, that was a fantastic letter. Brilliant!"

Hudson would ride me for the smallest things—insignificant typos and the like, complaining about how the document should not have gone to the client in that condition, as if the defect were material. But when I happened to review the memo of another associate and discovered several errors of law, he just brushed it off.

He scheduled quarterly reviews so that he could remind me of how poorly I was doing and reiterate that I wasn't going to make it at the firm. He wanted to make sure I got the message. He wanted to make sure I left. "It's time for your quarterly evaluation. Shall we set up lunch?"

"Yes," I said, and we made a date.

As noon approached on the appointed date, I waited in my office for him to come by. As I waited, Ted, another partner, walked past my office and stopped at the door to Hudson's. "Are you doing anything for lunch?" Ted inquired.

"No," Hudson replied.

Off they went. And there I sat, left to contemplate my unimportance.

I could never do enough, having to prove myself repeatedly. Right answers were quickly forgotten. Positives were either ignored or viewed as aberrations. Mistakes were exaggerated and emphasized (and, on occasion, fabricated), while accomplishments were cheapened.

It is amazing that African Americans who succeed in corporate America are able to perform better than most even though forced to spend so much time and energy just defending themselves, just trying to justify their existence, dealing with the constant pressure of feeling judged every minute—all the while competing against those who enjoy the luxury of unconditional acceptance. As poet Claudia

Rankine said, "The notable difference between black excellence and white excellence is that white excellence is achieved without having to battle racism. Imagine."

Once, I expressed concern to my supervising partner that I might be treated differently because I was black. He didn't get it. "Don't worry," he said. "We won't give you anything you don't deserve." I, of course, only wanted what I did deserve. I don't think he was trying to be an ass. He just didn't get it. Not surprisingly, his view of the world was that of a privileged white man.

I remember suffering through those early associate evaluations. A lot of moving of the goalposts, double-talk, false assumptions, and partners criticizing me, using words they couldn't pronounce properly, like "concomitant."

"We have discussed your progress at the firm. It is unacceptable, and we don't think that you are happy here."

"You are doing better, but you lack enthusiasm."

"You are very hard on the staff. You can't keep a secretary."

"You have complained about having to do scut work."

"You are disengaged."

"Disengaged." That was one of the better ones. They seldom engaged me, so that made me disengaged. I was told that I wasn't progressing like the others—the ones being taken along on client calls, going on business trips, and otherwise being drawn into the fold; the ones with whom the partners and the clients could more easily relate; the ones they did not presume incompetent.

I remember "discussing" my complaint that I had not been invited to attend the arbitration that I had worked on for six months. I argued that, at least in that instance, there should have been no dispute. I had spent a great deal of time researching and coming to grips with the underlying issues. Why couldn't I attend the actual proceeding? My arguments were met with calm indifference. I was told that my perception was wrong, that according to my supervising partner, I had been unavailable. In other words, it was my fault that I had not attended. It was my fault that my role had been diminished.

I tried to defend myself. I argued that I had indeed been available. "Perhaps you were," was the response, "but the partner perceived that you were not." My facts were dismissed, while the partner's perceptions became fact. I believe that what had really happened here is that the client had not wanted me at the proceeding, and so the partner went along. I didn't matter. What mattered was the fee.

I would hang around the office, available but underutilized, asking for work and waiting for the next opportunity. Not surprisingly, my hours were down. So the question was asked of me, with the appropriate innuendo, "Why are your hours down?" I would say nothing in reply. I said nothing because I couldn't think of anything to say. What was I supposed to say to counter the double-talk, the double standards, the unfairness of it all?

After my second annual debriefing, I was told that I was failing. Not good news. I asked my supervising partner for a meeting. I wanted an explanation. I wanted to discuss my future. I wanted someone to talk to. I wanted direction. But instead of helping, the partner avoided me. For weeks and months, he avoided me. We never did talk. Not once. Not ever. I called; I left notes. But he never responded. Never. Perhaps I wasn't worth the time. Perhaps he just plain as day did not care. Perhaps he felt guilty and didn't want to look me in the eye.

That's when I was transferred to Hudson. More than a month went by after my assignment to him before he gave me any work. Although he complained constantly of being overworked, he seldom assigned me anything. When I finally received something, it was busywork. "I need some work," I would say.

He would say, "Here's another file to organize. It's been years since anyone has looked at this one."

I wasn't learning anything. I complained, and I was told that the firm was not a law school.

I, of course, did not like being a file clerk. I had not gone to Yale to become a file clerk, much like the African Americans of my father's generation had not gone to college to be janitors and baggage handlers. When people outside the firm asked me what I did, I was embarrassed to tell them, so I didn't. I made stuff up. I lied and said that I was doing what my peers were doing. I adopted stories from their client meetings and their deals and their travels in an effort to maintain some modicum of self-esteem.

One time after I prepared a significant research memorandum for an important client, the client wrote a letter to the partner praising my work. The partner did not show me the letter, nor was it made a part of my file. That was the sort of evidence that was vigorously suppressed. The only reason I learned of the letter was that the partner's secretary, Dorothy, an older woman with a sense for what was right, brought it to me one day. God bless her. She knew what was going on, and it offended her sense of fairness.

She walked into my office, all business as she looked over her shoulder. "Hi, Dorothy," I said, greeting her with a smile.

Looking furtive, Dorothy didn't acknowledge the greeting. She just walked up to my desk and held out a letter from the general counsel of the client. "Here," she said, glum faced. "I thought that you would want to see this. I know that you would never see it otherwise." She turned and quickly left.

I read the letter.

Dear [Partner]:

Thank you for your letter of October 12 in the above itemizing your services, citing the hourly total, and also enclosing a copy of the memorandum recording the results of your research. I did indeed conclude that yours was a thorough and professional job. It has already made the rounds here, and much admiration has been expressed for it.

I take pleasure in enclosing our check payable to the order of your firm in the amount of your statement.

> [Client]
> [Officer]
> General Counsel

This was the general counsel's assessment of the significant research memorandum I had prepared for his company. And Dorothy was right—I never would have seen the letter but for her, as I never saw or heard about the letter again. The idea of clients being impressed with my work was something many of the partners in charge couldn't accept. In their minds, it just could not be true that I was capable of performing at a high level. Racist ideas were so firmly embedded in their souls that any assertion to the contrary, such as this general counsel's letter, had to be summarily dismissed—as would anything else contrary to the laws of physics.[51]

---

51 Of course, this behavior is consistent with the ingrained bias and attitudes that are integral to our society. We have a long tradition of ignoring or suppressing black achievement, a tradition so necessary to maintaining the myths of white supremacy and African American inferiority. For example, why did it take fifty-two years to award Vernon Baker the Medal of Honor? Why did the Tuskegee Airmen have to fight to fight? Why is it that hardly anyone is aware that the traffic signal was invented by an African American (let alone know his name, Garrett Morgan)? Or the automatic gearshift (Richard Spikes)? And there is so much we will never know, buried for all time—e.g., the exploits of black baseball players who toiled in obscurity in the Negro Leagues for their entire careers.

We would like to believe that no partner would think to suppress positive feedback about any associate,[52] just as we would like to believe that racism has been eradicated from our midst. "Sure, racism exists," people say, "but it is not practiced by anyone I know.[53] Sure, racism exists, but not in my organization. It is out there somewhere, but not around me." But if it hadn't been for Dorothy, I never would have seen that letter. The feedback was never mentioned when I was evaluated. The only thing I was told was that I could not write.

Once, a principal from one of Hudson's clients told me how much the company thought of me. After he finished, he closed with, "I am telling you this because I doubt that Hudson ever will." What was Hudson saying that made the client believe that he would never pass along to me a compliment?

I was in Nordstrom one day and bumped into a client of the firm, an older, white-haired gentleman. I never did any work for him, but we had run into each other in the

---

52 It is still suppression even if the partner believes that he is not suppressing positive information but instead ignoring information he sincerely believes, because of his unconscious bias, not to be true.

53 Often, white people who feel this way base their opinion of a certain individual on the way they are treated by her and on behavior they observe in nondiverse settings. They may know someone as genuinely nice, kind, and respectful to everyone in that nondiverse setting. The observer often fails even to consider the possibility that someone who appears so kind in the nondiverse setting may behave quite differently when confronted with African Americans or other minorities. Instead, when hearing stories of contrary behavior, the knee-jerk reaction is disbelief and denial.

office many times. Jokingly, he asked me why I was still at the firm. He thought I was in on the joke. I wasn't, but I pretended that I was. He told me that, given some of the things he had heard the partners say, he wondered why I hadn't left. I laughed awkwardly and said that I wondered the same thing. When I returned to the office, I had difficulty concentrating.

CHAPTER 12

Lurking beneath the Surface
(or in the Woodpile)

● ● ●

ONE OF MY BEST FRIENDS in law school was an African American named Paul Murphy. Paul ended up practicing in Boston, and for any number of reasons (his name, the absence of African Americans in major law firms, etc.), other lawyers dealing with him over the phone assumed he was white. One day, during a telephone conference with opposing counsel in a real estate deal, Paul was astonished when his fellow member of the Massachusetts bar exclaimed, "It was just like a nigger jumping out of a woodpile!"

Paul, in disbelief, murmured, "What?" The man then repeated himself. That sort of sentiment is often present, but its expression is usually more subtle.

One day, one of my partners and I were meeting with an officer of a company considering hiring our firm. My partner was white. The officer was a white male in his early forties. The officer explained his company to us, and we asked questions. We thought we understood, so we offered an analogy with the products of another company with which we were all familiar. The officer scoffed at the comparison. He replied, looking at my partner, "To compare their product to ours would be like comparing peaches"—he turned to me—"to watermelon."

Though I was perturbed, my expression remained unchanged. Perhaps I should have walked out of the room. My guess is that the executive wasn't conscious of his insult. His thoughts were second nature. Stereotypes bubbled up as naturally as breathing. With him, the black person is automatically seen in a negative light, subconsciously prejudged, and routinely denied opportunity. Needless to say, we were not hired. Even if it was beneath his awareness, the executive had no intention of ever hiring us the moment he saw me. I have experienced similar results any number of times when a potential client is referred to me – they seem to be attracted by my reputation and experience, only to grow cold upon seeing my face.

Further evidence of this powerful undercurrent of bigotry pulsating through American high society is provided by the attitude of a wealthy white man who served with me on the Cornish College of the Arts board of trustees. I had decided that, among other things, my role on the board would be to encourage diversity. The arts—what could be a less controversial setting in which to acknowledge, accept, and celebrate the genius of minorities? The myriad of brilliant contributions of artists of all races and backgrounds to music, theater, sculpture, painting, dance, and more cannot be seriously questioned. If there is one context in which the talent of blacks and other minorities, and the importance of their contributions, cannot be denied and dismissed as some product of affirmative action, it is the arts. But when I looked around the college, I saw very little diversity among the student body and the faculty. There wasn't much diversity on the board of trustees, either. Changes were required. But it would take time.

There was one change, however, that could be accomplished quickly. We could modify the curriculum. So I argued at a board of trustees meeting that the school should take immediate steps to modify the curriculum to better reflect the artistic contributions of persons of all races and cultures. At a minimum, the students should be made aware of the existence of those contributions and of the people who made them. To my dismay, one of the trustees spoke out against my proposal, which I had naïvely assumed to be benign. And it wasn't mild disapproval inviting legitimate debate. He found my idea repulsive, and he let it be known in no uncertain terms. In response to me, he raised his nose and arrogantly intoned, "We are not going to mongrelize the curriculum."

That was a first. I had never been called a mongrel before, at least not to my face. In essence, this man stood before the trustees of the college, many of Seattle's finest, and called me a nigger—and dared anyone to do anything about it. I was stunned. His contempt for me must have run pretty deep to allow for such a vitriolic, public, and ugly condemnation. Sadly, this was further confirmation of what I already knew to be true—that, notwithstanding the smiles, I was too often dismissed by those around me simply for being black.

I felt helpless and vulnerable. I had been there many times before: the only African American in a room full of privileged white people. Unexpectedly, someone drops a race bomb, and I am left alone to feel twenty pairs of eyes drilling into me—forty eyes trying to figure out my thoughts, wondering about my next move, outwardly showing concern but inwardly intrigued by the impending train wreck.

The words struck deeply. I wasn't standing on some street corner with someone yelling a racial epithet out the window of a car passing by. I was sitting in a boardroom surrounded by a group of well-educated, sophisticated college trustees. Without my provocative suggestion, I would have been none the wiser. I asked myself, *Can this really be happening?* It was surreal. As far as I knew, everyone in the room stood in agreement with that man. As far as I knew, they were secretly cheering him on. I groped for a reasoned response, but I was off balance, and nothing was making sense. Churning inside, I remained calm and started to speak, but before I could say much of anything, one of the other trustees stepped in and vigorously countered. He was the only one. No apologies were ever forthcoming from the offending trustee or from the college.

These episodes are a disturbing reminder of what is operating just beneath the surface in polite society, a reminder of why progress is so slow and why African American success can prove to be superficial and unenduring. There are those who just don't want diversity, don't believe in it, and cannot accept the idea that minorities are their equal. They don't want us around, or at least they don't want us too close. Further, too many of those who harbor such attitudes are in positions of power and influence. The fact that the Cornish College trustee was able to make such a statement in my presence with such ease made it all the more appalling and suggestive. Usually, such comments are reserved for times when no minority is within earshot. I could only imagine what he must say in private to his friends or to his children. It was the same sentiment expressed to me in a different way by a Seattle lawyer the summer after my second year in law school.

Prior to arriving in Seattle for a summer job following my second year of law school, I arranged to house-sit at the home of a local lawyer who was a senior associate at another large corporate law firm. He was taking time off for a long-anticipated vacation. We'll call him Gary. On the day of Gary's scheduled return, I vacated his home and moved elsewhere. Several days later, I returned to drop off his house keys. A small party was in progress, and Gary warmly invited me to stay and have a glass of wine.

All the guests were white; many of them were junior members of the bar. They all seemed welcoming. They all smiled and said the right things. They treated me like

I was one of them. There was a great deal of talking, with very little being said. Another pleasant summer evening was whiled away above Lake Washington, with Mount Rainier looming in the distance. All seemed right with the world.

As we stood around chatting, my host was spending an inordinate amount of time laughing at his own jokes and enjoying the attention. Going on and on, he related a story about an incredibly stupid thing he had done. He finished his story, quite satisfied with himself, and chuckled, "Ha, ha!" He laughed. "I felt as dumb as a darkie!"

Dumb as a darkie?

I fought to conceal my shock. Once again, I was being thrust onto center stage against my will as I became the recipient of unwelcome attention. Or so I thought. I was wrong.

I braced for the group's reaction, their rising as one to protest the racist remark. But the protest never came. Other than laughter, there was no reaction at all. For the others in the room, nothing had happened. By all appearances, this was all very normal, just words in common usage by those present. Nothing new, nothing unusual—an accurate reflection of the way they viewed African Americans. No one took offense. No one seemed to notice. Certainly, no one seemed to care, even with me present. Had I become that white, or was I just that invisible? More likely, concerning their racist attitudes or at least their unconscious bias, they all were simply that oblivious.

I surveyed the faces around the room smiling and laughing. The party hadn't skipped a beat. I no longer heard the music or anyone speaking. The moment was unreal. For me, the room spun out of control, but for everyone else, nothing was amiss. "How about those niggers? They sure can play ball. Would you like another glass of wine?"

I struggled to regain my balance on a deck that was now heaving and swaying in a storm generated by a surge of racism, or at least gross insensitivity. The others sipped their wine, oblivious to the turmoil in my world and secure on the solid footing of their own. In an instant, I went from feeling welcome to feeling merely tolerated. My face grew hot. No clever retort came to mind. I felt insignificant and trivial.

In time, I mustered a response. "Gary," I calmly said, "I may be dumb, but I'm smart enough to know when I'm not welcome and smart enough to have no desire to be here." I turned to leave.

All of the sudden, a collective lightbulb went on. Most everyone, belatedly, connected the dots, but they didn't know what to do about it. They just stood there, looking awkward. "Okay, Steve," said Gary, sheepishly. He walked me to the door, where we exchanged insincere good-byes. Gary never apologized.

If, indeed, he was sorry for what he said, I believe it was only because he had said it in my presence. As with so many others, for Gary, the racist speech was normal, second nature, and perfectly acceptable. The conscious or subconscious belief that "darkies" were dumb, and so much else, was intrinsic. Like so many of his colleagues, he had used the word or similar many times before, and he would use those words again. And sometimes, his children would hear him. And they would learn from him. They would learn, without understanding, that black people did not deserve respect. That black people were dumb. That it is okay to call them "darkies" or worse. This is the reality. These are the lessons that have been taught and passed down for generations, and they continue to be taught and passed down. These lessons help to ensure that the playing field remains anything but level.

CHAPTER 13

The Concept of Place

● ● ●

CENTRAL TO THE AMERICAN RACE problem is the concept of place, an enduring concept that has morphed over the years as it has stayed with us. Fundamentally, according to some, African Americans have a place in our society, usually subservient, and are expected to stay there or risk being considered an "uppity nigger" and forced to pay the consequences.[54] This has not changed. What has changed is the perception of what that place is, and that, in turn, is defined by the one doing the perceiving. But whatever the place, if an African American steps out of it, he becomes a target, someone to be ostracized or otherwise taken down a notch or two at the first opportunity—or at least someone to be annoyed with for failing to follow the rules.

For many, the ultimate example of a black man forgetting his place is Barack Obama. For those who feel this

---

54 This way of thinking, of course, is a reflection of the ideas of white supremacy that underpin American culture, one of the many aspects of American history that we don't like to talk about or even acknowledge fully.

way, the idea of a black family living in the White House was too much, prompting violent, irrational, almost insane reactions. Many who have reacted negatively to President Obama simply due to the color of his skin were among the same people who for years had proclaimed America the land of opportunity, where anyone could grow up to be president. They felt safe expressing such an open-minded point of view because they were secure in their belief that a black man would never seriously contend for the presidency.

As in the case of Barack Obama and countless other lesser situations, African American progress is deemed to be fine—just don't take it too far. The majority has been conditioned to expect African Americans to occupy positions of servitude, not leadership.[55] Some, when confronting African Americans in positions of wealth and authority exceeding theirs, suddenly find their world out of alignment, resulting in disorientation and animosity derived from feelings of impotency.

I am reminded of the time when my father, who was a civil-engineering professor at Iowa State University, overheard our white Iowa neighbors say to their backyard guests, "Those are educated niggers. You can't push them around." Similarly, though perhaps less blatant, I have seen

---

[55] I cannot remember all of the places where those present assumed I was there to serve them. I attended a reception at the Seattle Tennis Club, and a man asked me to get him a drink. I was standing at my table with my family in a restaurant, and a man at the reception desk motioned for me to come over and help him. It goes on and on.

white associates and white partners who, I believe, were perfectly fine with my presence in their law firm but who bristled when finding themselves having to answer to me. Among other things, as a partner, I have had white associates slam my office door because I sent documents to a client without the associate's review, snatch a document from my hands and stomp out of my office in response to my critique, and ignore my directions (thereby placing a client's security interest in jeopardy)—all things no associate interested in advancing his career would do unless he deemed the partner to be of no consequence.

Similarly, I have had white partners disregard my position in the firm and proceed on matters within my jurisdiction as if I did not exist. In short, these individuals were perfectly fine accepting me as a human being, but as a leader or as a person in a position of authority over them, my legitimacy was questioned.

A friend of mine, an African American, while heading up human relations for a major corporation, required some top-level accounting assistance. He phoned one of his buddies at a large accounting firm, another African American. His friend assured him that his firm had the required expertise and offered to send over two of his partners. The two partners were white. Back at his office, my friend waited in a conference room for the accountants. When the accounting firm partners entered the conference room, they saw only my friend. They stopped, excused themselves, and left. They eventually sorted out the situation and crawled back. Although perturbed, my friend went ahead and hired the accounting firm, but only because he didn't want to hurt his buddy. Similarly, I was once sent to a major client for a meeting and upon arrival was directed to a conference room. When the officer I was sent to interview arrived, he stopped at the door and said, "Oh, excuse me. I am looking for our lawyer." He then turned and left.[56]

I remember being in the copy room as a third-year associate at my first law firm; enter a visiting lawyer from a Wall Street firm. White, pushing forty. He sized me up immediately. "Make three copies for me," he ordered, handing me a thick document.

I smiled and took the document. "Sure," I said. I often made a game of the assumptions people made.

While the copies were running, one of the partners with whom the New York lawyer was working walked in. "Hello, Steve," he called out to me, smiling.

The visiting lawyer turned to the partner. "I will be right with you," he said. "Your file-room guy is running a couple of copies for me," he continued, nodding toward me.

The partner's face reddened as his smile evaporated. His eyes caught mine. I just shrugged my shoulders. "He's not our file-room guy," the partner said awkwardly. "He is one of our associates."

---

56 In these cases, initially there is no shock that the lawyer or high-level executive is a black man, because the automatic assumption is that the black man is not the lawyer or high-level executive. Their underlying bias corrects for the discrepancy; the shock comes later.

The New York lawyer showed a hint of surprise but offered no apology, only a thin smile and a subtle nod. He had been thrown off. Where he came from, if you were black, it was usually a safe bet that you weren't one of the lawyers. Instead, you were likely to be the one going from office to office, shining shoes. He took his copies and left.

I was standing outside of San Francisco International Airport, waiting for my driver to pick me up and take me to a board of directors meeting for a client. As I stood there, a white woman approached me. She fiddled in her handbag in search of money while mumbling something. The scene unfolding was unexpected, so I was slow to pick up on what was transpiring. Thinking that the woman wanted directions, I shifted my focus and gave her my full attention. Suddenly, she made it clear that she wanted me to help her with her luggage, thrusting some dollars in my direction. *Oh, here we go again*, I said to myself. "Do you think I work here?" I asked the woman.

She looked at me as if to say, "What else would you be doing here?" It then dawned on her that maybe I wasn't a porter, and she unapologetically moved on.

Once, I found myself waiting with one of my legal assistants for the valet to bring around my car after a dinner celebrating the closing of a significant transaction for one of my clients. A white man approached us and tried to give me his valet ticket. He looked at me without seeing me. I stared at him, not saying a word but sending a clear, nonverbal message. After a moment, he seemed to see my face for the first time. He grew fearful, shrinking back, one stereotype taking over for another.

Mobile, Alabama, during World War II offers a good example of how the concept of place operates. Prior to the war, blacks and whites got along just fine, provided the blacks kept their place. When wartime jobs enabled African Americans to buy nice homes and drive nice cars, trouble started. African Americans were not supposed to own nice homes and drive nice cars. That upset the balance of nature. Although the contexts may differ, this theme continues to be played out today. Those who continue to fight against full acceptance are often annoyed by the success of the black person who has dared step outside of his place and elevate himself to a position, to an income level, thought to be reserved for whites.

I am reminded of a banker I talked to when trying to get a loan to buy my current home. At the time, I was a partner at the largest law firm in Seattle and on a good trajectory in terms of career path. Notwithstanding all the positives, the banker, an older white man, rejected my loan application. As a matter of substance, there should have been no issue (of course, the bank that eventually loaned me the money saw no issue), but arguably, I didn't fit neatly within the bank's guidelines. I challenged the banker's decision. The key facts were in my favor, so it was a difficult debate for him. During our discussion, he grew tense. Finally, emotion getting the better of him, he showed his hand by blurting out, "Why, my son can't even afford a house like that!" Until that moment, the thought that race might be motivating the banker's thinking had not entered my mind, but suddenly, it all seemed clear. The real issue for the banker was not my qualifications, but the fact that I was trying to acquire a prime piece of real estate that, in the banker's world, I had no business owning. The banker's decision was based not on the merits, but upon what his son could and could not have. This is the sort of blatant racism that too often stands firmly in the path to African American success, silent and invisible, rendering the merits irrelevant and leaving African Americans to wonder why things don't go right even with what should be favorable odds.

In many ways, the real issue is competition. For some, elimination of competition to the fullest extent possible, even down to their own colleagues, is the primary objective. As individuals seek to limit competition, African Americans are an easy target. Fundamentally, not much has changed over the years. Consider this. During the elections of 1862, in denouncing the Emancipation Proclamation, Democratic Party resolutions denounced "the Black Republican 'party of fanaticism' that intended to free 'two or three million semi-savages' to 'overrun the North and enter competition with the laboring white masses.'"[57] Competition. We speak more politely today, but we say the same things.

---

57 James M. McPherson, *Antietam: Crossroads of Freedom*, Oxford University Press (2002), 147.

Also during the elections of 1862, "midwestern Democratic orators proclaimed that 'every white man in the North who does not want to be swapped off for a free Nigger, should vote the Democratic ticket.'"[58] The leading Democratic newspaper in New York, the *World*, declared that a vote for the Democrat running for governor of New York would be "a vote to protect our white laborers against association and competition of Southern Negroes."[59] Competition and association.

There is little substantive difference between the sentiment expressed in 1862 and that expressed today by opponents of diversity and affirmative action or that reflected in the actions taken by those who can always find a reason to disqualify the African American. It seems that in too many ways, the only thing that has changed in 150-plus years is how we say things—not what we say, or what we do, or why we do it. The underlying thinking remains the same. We have just repackaged it for a more tolerant society, or, depending on your point of view, a society less tolerant of overt racism but quite accepting of the subtle variety, or at least complacent about it.

For these reasons, I disappointed a lot of people when I got into Yale. In fact, there were those who were unhappy when I was accepted by lesser schools. Greater success only brought greater animosity.

---

58 Ibid.
59 Ibid.

The first law school I heard from was Boston University. When I received my acceptance letter, I shared the happy news with a friend, a fellow political science major, who happened to be white. The friend had also applied to law school and was waiting to hear something from anyone. Upon hearing my news, he didn't congratulate me or wish me well. "I don't plan on having to settle for such a poor law school," was all he could muster.

He then murmured something about his little sister having trouble getting into the college of her choice because of all the blacks they were admitting. The friend's face grew cold, no longer reflecting the friendship that had been so evident moments before. I allowed the conversation to sputter to an end. We parted and never again discussed law schools or otherwise shared our dreams. In fact, we didn't discuss much of anything after that. We drifted apart. He couldn't deal with my success. He couldn't deal with African American success. To the extent African Americans were assigned places in top law schools, to the extent African Americans obtained good jobs, he saw the chances for his own success, and that of his family, diminished. Every desirable position held by an African American meant one less desirable position for a white person. To him, that was unacceptable.

Competition is fine until minorities participate. Then suddenly, it becomes a zero-sum game. It is another way of saying the same old thing: only whites may play; blacks need not apply. Of course, the exclusion of all African Americans from elite colleges or from top jobs would not necessarily result in an offer letter for the complaining member of the majority, but somehow, that complaining member would feel better about it.

I paid for college living expenses by working in a machine shop with a group of blue-collar white men mostly from rural Iowa. Although over the years, I had won the respect of most of the men on the shop floor and they were pleased with my success, sharing in it as if it were their own,[60] the assistant foreman was cut from a different cloth. He saw himself as important and someone special, and he saw me as something of a nightmare. "This is in your blood," he would taunt me. "You're not going anywhere." He predicted that I would always be in that shop for him to order around, that I would never graduate from college. But his dream was slipping away. It appeared that I was moving on, advancing through life in a way that seemed to trouble him.

One day, I found myself working in his office, which doubled as a conference room. I was organizing stacks of forms on a large table. The assistant foreman stood behind

---

60 Many of the men on that shop floor had never interacted with a black man before, and when I arrived, I was put in that special place in their minds reserved for black people. It wasn't a good place. After close association for nearly four years, the majority of them changed their view of me. Instead of a member of a group they had been taught to hate or at least to disrespect, I became an individual. More than one of them assured me that if I returned to Ames, Iowa, and they ever needed a lawyer, they would look to hire me. They even took up a collection to help with my expenses, and they made it clear that in their minds, I was different from other blacks. This was meant as a compliment.

his desk, staring. He studied me but said nothing. After a while, he spoke. "So I hear you are going to law school," he sneered. He made it sound as if he thought that I was being a little uppity.

"Yes, sir," I said. "I am going to law school."

The assistant foreman shook his head and sat down in his chair. He leaned back and swiveled slowly from side to side. As I continued with my work, he watched, trying to sort things out. He seemed bothered, almost bewildered. After a bit, a thin smile crept across his wrinkled face. He had an idea, a way to put me back in my place. "Well, then, where are you going? Harvard or Yale?"

He chuckled, pleased with himself and his little joke. *He may be going to law school*, he thought, *but at least he isn't going to a good law school.* Certainly, that wasn't possible. And whatever law school I entered, he could always remind me that it wasn't Harvard or Yale. That was his putdown, his ticket to feeling good about himself. He could always cheapen my accomplishment by reminding me that I wasn't going to Harvard or Yale.

I stopped shuffling papers and looked up. I didn't know what to say. I examined my cards. Harvard…Yale. I thought about how best to play my hand. A good comeback eluded me. Unsmiling, I met his eyes. The old man smirked from behind his desk. "Zing!" he exclaimed, chuckling, full of self-satisfaction.

After a moment, I shrugged and returned to my work. As I picked up another batch of forms, I said, "Where am

I going? Harvard or Yale? I don't know; I haven't decided yet. I got into both."

The simple truth was devastating. The assistant foreman nearly fell over backward, visibly stunned. He knew I wasn't lying. "Damn," he said under his breath, frowning. "Goddamn."

Other than that, he was speechless. The expression on his face was a look of confused hate. I caught the look out of the corner of my eye, and it frightened me. I never forgot that moment. I was learning. As an African American, I was coming to the realization that I had to be prepared to be disliked merely for being successful. I was beginning to understand the destructive potential of jealousy combined with bigotry.

It is hard to get away from this whole idea of place. On a lighter note, United Airlines once tried to remove me from my seat so a white man could have it. I was traveling from Chicago to Seattle. They were still flying DC-10s at the time, and I favored the first-row window—plenty of legroom and the sense that you were the only person on the plane. I boarded and took my seat: 1A. As I settled in, a white man, someone I had never seen before, took the seat next to me: 1B. We put our things away, pulled out some reading material, slightly reclined our seats, and set about relaxing as the rest of the plane boarded.

A little later, another white man appeared. He hovered over 1B and me for a few seconds, and then he sought my attention. I noticed him out of the corner of my eye but chose to ignore him. Finally, the man leaned over and tapped me on the shoulder. I looked up. "You are in my seat," he said to me.

My first thought was that I had screwed up. "Sorry," I said, reaching into my shirt pocket for my boarding stub. I reexamined it. I hadn't screwed up; it said *1A*. "Ah," I said, smiling at the stranger. "It looks like I'm in the right place." I flashed the stub at him and then returned it to my pocket.

The stranger wasn't giving up easily. He fumbled with his carry-ons, letting his suit bag fall to the floor. Fishing in his pockets, he eventually produced his own boarding stub. By now, he was beet red and breathing heavily. As it turned out, his stub also said *1A*. He shoved the evidence in my face and waited for me to get up. I leaned away but otherwise didn't move. I reproduced my own stub and allowed the stranger to take a closer look. "Seems like we both have been assigned 1A," I said. "Lucky for me, I got here first."

I flashed a smile that wasn't reciprocated. The stranger studied my stub, standing motionless as he processed the information.

"I will take that back, if you don't mind?" I said after a moment. The stranger returned the stub, casting a glare my way surely designed to make me combust. I didn't combust but instead shifted in my seat and returned to my book. I pretended to read and tried to ignore the still-hovering stranger. He clenched and unclenched his fists, contemplating his next move. *Just go away*, I thought. Ultimately, the stranger threw up his hands and retreated in a huff.

Peace restored, 1B and I went back to our reading. Peace was short-lived.

Within minutes, the man reappeared with reinforcements in the form of the gate agent, a short white woman with the bearing of a drill sergeant accustomed to barking orders and being obeyed. The stranger wore the silly grin of a schoolboy anticipating his reward for kissing up to the teacher. As the agent sized up the situation, the stranger smiled from a safe distance. He had me now! He and his newfound ally were going to show me a thing or two.

The gate agent leaned over 1B and, unsmiling, said to me, "You are in this man's seat," pointing at the stranger.

I was somewhat startled. There was no introduction. No "Let's determine the facts." No "May I see your boarding pass?" No offer to hear my side of the story. No request for evidence that might support my right to be in seat 1A. Just a terse "You are in this man's seat!"

How had the agent reached her decision so quickly and with so few facts? Why was it that no further inquiry was necessary? Did she think that I was just some crazy man who walked onto airplanes and sat wherever he pleased? She provided no support or explanation for her conclusion. I was simply to leave because some other man wanted my seat.

It reminds me of the time on another United Airlines flight when the flight attendant barred me from the first-class restroom even though I was sitting in first class. She just assumed I didn't belong. In response to my rejection, I said, "Okay," and retreated toward the restrooms at the rear of the plane, assuming that for some reason the first-class restroom was unavailable at that moment. I had been too naïve and accepting to appreciate that something was amiss. It was an older white woman in the last row of first class, however, who had been paying attention. As I passed by, she caught my eye and asked, "Why won't she let you use that restroom?" She had picked up on something I had missed, perhaps a gesture behind my back.

My own mind shifted gears. *Yes*, I said to myself, *why isn't she letting me use the restroom?* I smiled at the woman, shrugged my shoulders, walked back to the flight attendant, and popped the question. "Why can't I use this restroom?"

She looked at me as one might look at a child who just can't seem to comprehend that what he is doing is wrong. "This restroom is for people sitting up here," the flight attendant answered, emphasizing "up here" as if to help me to understand. She didn't ask where I was sitting; she didn't have to. She knew I didn't belong.

This is reminiscent of yet another United Airlines flight. I was traveling from LA to Honolulu with my wife and three children. We were flying first class (all part of the deal, as we had just flown in from Paris in business class). They called for first-class boarding, but when we tried to get on, we were barred, the assumption being that we were not in first class. But I digress. Back to the stranger who wanted seat 1A.

I met the eyes of the gate agent with calm defiance. I handed her my boarding stub. She examined it and confirmed that it said *1A*. For a moment, she seemed uncertain, but then just as quickly, she dismissed the evidence—a standard practice. If the facts aren't working for you, ignore them. She returned my stub and proclaimed, "You will have to leave."

I raised my left eyebrow. What rule was being applied here? I had been assigned the seat by the airline, but apparently, that wasn't enough. The airline had made a mistake, so I had to leave even though I had been the first to arrive. There was no acknowledgement that I was actually sitting in my assigned seat, neither was there any explanation of why the stranger should have the seat instead of me. Under the circumstances, I had no intention of giving up. "I'm not going anywhere," I said as pleasantly as I could. "Not my problem."

Meanwhile, 1B had been taking in the unfolding melodrama. He had sized up the situation while trying to read his book and had drawn his own conclusions. He quietly weighed in. Without lifting his eyes, he tilted his head slightly toward me and, without moving his lips, whispered, "Stay." A small gesture, perhaps, but a telling one. Suddenly, I had an ally in this little skirmish. I felt empowered.

The gate agent didn't have any answers, so she tried raising her voice. "You will have to leave," she repeated more forcefully. "You are in this man's seat." Being louder did nothing for the strength of her argument.

"I'm not persuaded," I said.

"Stay," whispered 1B.

"I'm not moving," I said firmly, smiling all the while.

"This man has been assigned that seat," argued the gate agent.

"So have I!" I replied.

"Stay," whispered 1B. "Stay."

The stranger's look of juvenile glee turned to concern. Things were not going according to plan.

"Look, I didn't issue this boarding pass to myself," I said. "Your airline assigned me this seat and, really, until you come up with something better than just 'Get out,' I have no intention of leaving."

Frustrated and angry that she could not move me with her barking, the gate agent whispered something to my antagonist and retreated, presumably to gather reinforcements. The man stayed behind, shifting his weight from one foot to the other and casting an occasional impotent glare my way. 1B buried his nose in his book.

The gate agent returned, alone. She avoided eye contact with me as she produced a fistful of flight coupons and negotiated a settlement with the stranger. A deal was struck, and they both retreated.

The whole incident served as a metaphor for what I experience far too often, only the stakes are usually considerably higher than a seat on an airplane. I do wish I had asked the whisperer's name.

CHAPTER 14

Leveling the Playing Field after the Fact

● ● ●

As a race, African Americans have been beaten, battered, bought, sold, starved, robbed, and marginalized. They have been raped and murdered with impunity for centuries—stripped of their humanity by a society in search of ways to justify injustice and ease the collective conscience. Remarkably, we are told, there are no lingering effects from all of this. Racism, we are to believe, is a thing of the past. Today, with everything corrected and protective laws in place, African Americans are figuratively dumped at the starting line in a broken heap and invited to compete as equals, receiving assurances that henceforth, reward will be allocated purely on the merits. Occupying a position of weakness more than three hundred years in the making, we are supposed to rejoice at the equality we now enjoy and pretend that the pervasive bias operating against us at every level has gone the way of slave ships and lunch-counter sit-ins. It is a construct designed to preserve the status quo for as long as possible.

For minorities, reaching the top and staying there is exceedingly difficult. The difficulty is often unappreciated by whites, indeed often unnoticed by minorities, as the harsh reality continues as the accepted norm. Circumstances are made worse by the blind offensive against affirmative action that provides the needed excuse for many to justify effectively turning their backs on diversity and inclusion, casting an eye backward and longing for the days when *Plessy v. Ferguson*[61] was the law of the land. With righteous fervor, they are given license to speak with just-sounding words that, when decoded, in reality decry the notion of maximizing opportunity for the historically disenfranchised and turn a blind eye to historical and current fact.

The opponents of affirmative action are further supported and given strength by a few prominent African Americans—and some not so prominent—who seem to have very short memories or very poor eyesight and are only too willing to subscribe to the biases of the majority. Those who speak against taking affirmative steps to address lingering bias are able to pretend that all is fair and that the playing field is now actually level. In this fantasyland of self-delusion, prejudice no longer exists and African Americans need only to work hard and, with the same amount of effort, all things now being equal, they will reap the same rewards, have the same opportunities,

---

61 *Plessy v. Ferguson* is the 1896 US Supreme Court case that upheld the constitutionality of segregation under the "separate but equal" doctrine. The vote was seven justices in favor, one justice not present. The case resulted from the jailing of a thirty-year-old African American, Homer Plessy, for sitting in the "white" car of the East Louisiana Railroad.

and receive the same compensation for the same work as their white counterparts. We are to believe all these things because others whose clarity of sight is far greater than our own have declared them to be so. For me, however, reality is not so easily dismissed.

One of the more insidious aspects of this little game is that it works to solidify stereotypes. After all, if the playing field is really level, then minority underperformance can only be attributed to minority shortcomings.

Significant leveling has occurred, but the job is far from finished. Continued affirmative action is required. Unfortunately, the mere mention of affirmative action triggers in many an extreme visceral reaction. Like so many efforts to improve society over the years, affirmative action has lost its original meaning and is being pushed aside, largely as the result of inflammatory terminology such as "race-based preferences" and "reverse discrimination."[62]

Those who attack affirmative action programs broadly have little appreciation for its original intent or the continued existence of bias and how it operates to tilt the field against minorities, or perhaps they simply have little desire

---

62 Essentially, affirmative action in the United States began on March 6, 1961, when President John F. Kennedy issued Executive Order 10925. The order provided in part that government contractors "take affirmative action to ensure that applicants are employed, and employees are treated during employment, without regard to their race, creed, color or national origin." It affirmed the government's commitment to equal opportunity for all qualified persons, taking positive action to strengthen efforts to realize true equal opportunity for all.

to change the status quo. In either case, the argument seems to be that affirmative action programs are nothing more than programs to advance people other than on the basis of merit, to the detriment of the group that has held all the cards of privilege for the past three hundred years or more. Society's heart has grown a little colder as we have allowed the notion of affirmative action to be corrupted.

One evening while working late, I engaged a white associate in a debate on affirmative action. He picked his way around the issues, trying hard not to offend. He failed. The few African American students in attendance at his law school, according to him, were products of affirmative action and had not belonged.

"The black students were out of their depth," he argued. "The ones who were there should not have been admitted. For example, not one black student was on law review. This shows that the black students didn't have it." Usually, only the best and the brightest law students are chosen to serve on a school's law review, its top legal periodical for scholarly writing.

I considered the logic. "Was every white student on law review?"

The associate answered me with silence.

"So," I asked, "how many black students were there? Ten? So ten black students were not on law review? How many white students were *not* on law review?"

More silence.

I said, "So, just a guess, but I would say that there were many more white students not on law review than there

were black students not on law review. So I don't understand your point. I don't think the absence of black students on law review proves anything except, perhaps, the
existence of bias. Or maybe they found the whole idea an
unappealing bore."

There was no attempt to counter.

"And, just for the fun of it," I added, "are there any
other ways of measuring smarts and predicting success, or
just your way?"

There are two fundamental problems associated with
the notion of affirmative action today. First, as I have
stated, we have managed to give it a bad name by twist-
ing and distorting the act of assisting those still burdened
by institutional and systemic racism into something un-
American. Equity and fairness in this context has somehow become a zero-sum game.[63] We have allowed cries to
end the ingrained subconscious bias, blatant bigotry, and
everything in between to be drowned out by the shouts
condemning so-called "reverse discrimination" and "race-
based preferences."[64] We are left with an uphill fight as
affirmative action, burdened by the negative labels and a

---

63 It is interesting to note that, too often, white individuals argue that
a minority holding a job has taken it from someone more deserving.
They seldom resort to such rhetoric if the job is held by another white
person.

64 Affirmative action as a purported tool for discriminating against
whites hasn't been very effective. Look no further than the rolls of equity partners in major law firms, the boards of directors of important
corporations, and the executives managing those corporations.

new set of rules designed, we are told, to "ensure fairne͟ recedes, leaving bias in all its forms more entrenched.

The second fundamental problem has to do with the diversity illusion. We cite African Americans holding high office or less lofty, but still important, positions in corporate America and other sectors of society in support of the argument that affirmative action is not even necessary. Diversity and fairness have been achieved and, therefore, our work here is done.

True, there has been change. We are no longer at zero, as a group, but little else can be said. Unfortunately, there are just enough of us around in high places to create the illusion of diversity, just enough to make those who are not paying close attention believe that everything is okay and that we are progressing quite nicely as a nation, just enough to support the argument that nothing more needs to be done.

And there are those who are not so disingenuous as to argue that we have arrived but instead are of the view that diversity and inclusion, and the eradication of the bias so deeply rooted in our society, will somehow take care of themselves without affirmative action if we just leave well enough alone. Perhaps the most troubling of this group are the minorities who have managed to achieve a high level of success (often as the result of affirmative action) but who are distressed because they feel that affirmative action programs somehow stigmatize their achievements. Now that they are successful, it is time to end all consideration of race in admissions and employment. All of those less fortunate, less

ls who would make it but for the fact that
e and well will just have to work harder.

twofold: first, we must accept the fact
that implicit and explicit bias continue to play a significant
role in denying minorities equal opportunity. Second, we
must develop affirmative-action programs that effectively
end or neutralize that bias.

Despite all the good intentions, many affirmative-action programs have indeed missed the mark. Affirmative
action isn't, or at least it shouldn't be, a means to move anyone forward other than on her merits. Taking an extreme
example, insisting on quotas would create opportunity for
some, but when I think of creating equal opportunity, that
is not the sort of thing I have in mind. Affirmative action
cannot mean establishing quotas or dropping standards.
That would not be leveling the playing field; that would be
throwing the game. We don't change society for the better
by declaring as the winner the man with one hand tied behind his back. We change society for the better by untying
that hand and allowing that man to compete fairly. This
means acknowledging bias, especially the unconscious variety, and finding meaningful ways to counter it. It means
that when determining whether an individual meets the
standards, it may be necessary and appropriate to go beyond traditional criteria. There usually is more than one
test that can be appropriately applied in any given situation
to determine ability or to predict success.

Affirmative action should be nothing more than help,
a means of creating opportunity for those who don't have

others out in front clearing the way and opening doors for them. It should be help for those who might not otherwise have a chance because of the deeply rooted prejudice that continues to afflict the hearts and minds of a majority of the majority, at least at some level; help in forcing a change in attitudes that otherwise would go unchanged, challenging views of the world that would otherwise go unchallenged; help with the goal of creating diversity and opportunity where they are limited or nonexistent—a means of fighting the subtle undercurrent of racism that is often unseen and therefore deemed not to exist.

We need to be clever about developing programs designed to fundamentally address the lingering effects of slavery and Jim Crow—programs that are designed to once and for all eradicate the undercurrent of bias in our country or at least reduce it to levels where it is no longer significant. We need programs that are designed to ensure that every child has a good education, meaningful healthcare, and proper nourishment; and programs that ensure that every man, woman, and child willing to put in the effort is equipped to compete and then allowed to compete. No self-respecting people want handouts. They just don't want the door barred. No African American wants to be hired because he is black – he just doesn't want to be not hired because he is black.

In the end, we are where we began: the collision between equal opportunity (the ideal) and discrimination (the reality). Until opportunity is truly equal and until discrimination is truly absent, we need appropriately structured programs designed to recognize, acknowledge, and correct for bias. Perhaps, though, we should not call these programs "affirmative action," as that has become such a loaded term. Perhaps we should just call these measures what they would be—antibias programs.[65] I would hope that most Americans are not reluctant to think in those terms.

---

65 Affirmative action is known as *employment equity* in Canada, *reservation* in India and Nepal, and *positive discrimination* in the United Kingdom.

CHAPTER 15

Up Stares, Down Stares

● ● ●

I ROUTINELY DRAW STARES. I walk into a conference room, and there is the guy who can't stop staring. Does he think he knows me? Is he staring in disbelief that an African American is in the room? Is he pleased? Is he displeased? It can be annoying.

But it's not always negative. Once, two white ladies in a restaurant in New York stopped me and asked, "Are you famous?"

I said, "Not yet."

Or the time a white man eased up to me in an airport and asked, "Should I know you?"

I can never know exactly why people stare. I just know that they do.

One night when visiting Sirmione in Northern Italy with my family, our son wasn't feeling well, so my wife sent me and our oldest daughter, Aimee, into town to find dinner for ourselves. She stayed back at the Villa Cortine Palace with the other kids. Aimee, who was eight at the time, and I wound up at a little trattoria on a tiny side street with a nice view of Lake Garda. We were shown to a table next to a window. As I perused the menu, I couldn't help but notice a woman across the room staring at us. I tried to ignore her.

"What do you want for dinner?" I asked Aimee as she sat there all prim and proper like the little princess she was.

"Do they have anything I would like?" she asked in turn.

I glanced in the direction of the staring woman and noticed that she was talking to her dinner companion and nodding in our direction. I was a bit puzzled, but I put it out of my mind and turned my attention to Aimee. We eventually settled on dinner and placed our order.

As we waited for our dinner to arrive, the staring woman abruptly rose from her chair and headed in our direction. I watched as she weaved her way through the other tables, sizing her up as she approached. American. White. Between forty-five and fifty. Fit and seemingly wealthy. She would have been at home shopping in Palm Beach or Beverly Hills.

She stopped at our table. *Well?* I thought, waiting for her to say something. Aimee seemed mystified. Was this another waitress?

"Pardon me," she said, "but I just had to come and talk to you. If I go back to the States and tell my son that I saw you and didn't talk to you and get your autograph, he would never forgive me!"

I looked at her with my left eyebrow raised. *Here we go again*, I said to myself. *Which professional athlete has she decided I must be?*

"Now," she said, explaining all, "what is your name? I mean, I know you play basketball, but I can't remember your name."

Tall black man at Lake Garda—must be a basketball player.

"I don't play basketball," I said for what must have been the millionth time in my life. I was too taken aback to think of a clever response. Only later did it dawn on me that I should have given her the name of a white player to proudly take back to her son.

Now looking befuddled, the woman stammered something that might have been interpreted as, "Well, then, who in the hell are you?" She acted as if I had played a trick on her. It was my fault that I had failed to somehow identify myself as not a professional athlete.

"I'm just a lawyer from Seattle," I said.

Discovering that I was just a regular black guy, she now wanted no part of me. It was as if it was okay to be seen with a famous black man, but an ordinary one, not so much. "Excuse me," she said as she made a hasty retreat.

Something similar happened in a little restaurant in Florence, Italy. We ran into two couples from New Jersey, probably in their midfifties. White. One man was much too fat, wearing shorts much too tight and much too short. He claimed to be a judge. After the obligatory stare-a-thon, they approached us and began their cross-examination. They were trying to figure out what I was doing in Florence, where, apparently, no African American man should be. "Do you play basketball?" No. "Are you in the army?" No. I never did give them any real answers, forcing them to slink away scratching their heads.

There are the more pleasant times, like when I encountered a little Italian boy at the showers on the beach in Marina di Pietrasanta. He saw me and excitedly started to move as if he was dribbling a basketball, speaking to me in rapid-fire Italian that I could not possibly understand. He seemed to think that I was somebody special, and I seemed to have made his day, and that was okay.

All that said, the remark to me by a young African American man I bumped into on a downtown Seattle street exemplifies the broad reach of stereotypes. He sized me up and asked, "Hey, man, do you still have that jump shot?"

CHAPTER 16

Compensation Funny Business

● ● ●

To RECEIVE LESS FOR THE same or greater work isn't fair, but it is the system. I know that, and I even accept it. The glass is more than half full. Indeed, I determined early on that in corporate America, a black man's primary goal must be survival—simply staying on the playing field and living to fight another day. The primary goal cannot be winning fair treatment (although fair treatment should always be encouraged). That would be a nice outcome, but, I am afraid, that would be asking too much.

It would have been a waste of time, and not good for my mental health, to worry too much about any disparity between what I believed I had earned and what I actually received. Nothing was going to change, at least not near term. Moreover, I was being paid much more than most everyone else in the world, so as long as I was having fun, I didn't really care. In the end, I was grateful just to be a player, hence my primary goal of simply remaining in the game and not worrying too much about whether the referees were calling it fairly. Occasionally, however, one of my partners would worry about unfairness directed my way.

I was serving on the Perkins partner compensation committee and sitting through another tedious meeting assessing and debating each partner's individual performance, when one of my partners leaned over and whispered to me. She was wondering about a partner we will just call Herman. "There is something I am trying to figure out," she said. "I look at Herman's compensation and what he has done, and I don't understand why he is more highly compensated than you. If anything, you have accomplished more, yet your compensation is less. Can you explain to me what's going on here?"

"I cannot," I said. "I asked the same question for years. I have stopped asking. It's just the way it is. You are welcome to pursue it if you would like, but Herman is not the only example. If you analyze many of the numbers, some of the disparities are quite striking."

"I will pursue it," she said in earnest. Not much happened after that. She met with the same brick wall.

Later, just before I left the firm, I received a big bump in pay with a comment from the managing partner to the effect that it was great that the firm was at last in a position to pay me what I was worth. I am pretty sure that the firm had the money all along. It was a welcome gesture, but too late.

While serving another stint on the Perkins partner compensation committee, I was inadvertently given additional insight into the nature of the machinations employed behind the scenes in an effort to tamp down my compensation and standing in the firm. It is one thing to have unconscious bias that works to blind one to African American skills and accomplishments, but it is something altogether different for someone to mount a concerted campaign to denigrate, complete with fabrications designed to play into the stereotypes.

As part of the partner compensation process, comments were solicited from every partner on every other partner. This information, along with a great deal of statistical and other data, was then assembled in several volumes of notebooks. Each partner on the committee was given a set of notebooks that required extensive study over the Thanksgiving weekend. All the notebooks were identical except that each partner's set of notebooks had deleted from it comments of other partners regarding him or her.

My notebooks had not been properly filtered this time. I had been given the comments of one of the senior partners in my group about me. They reminded me that some partners remained unhappy or annoyed with my success and were proactively engaged in trying to push me back.

I discovered these comments late one night as I was poring over the reams of material and forming opinions of the performance of each of my partners. There the words were—right to the heart. I was still a target to be singled out for gratuitous mischief. I was described as a malcontent, a person filled with hostility, a person who was going to be difficult to keep busy, a management challenge:

Steve Graham. Steve will always pitch in and help out on anything. Some of his traditional clients may be winding down some of their big efforts, and it will be a challenge to make sure Steve's work continues. Steve has built up residual hostility and aggravation about the compensation system. It will require some management skills to keep him positive. He has a sense of grievance which has not gone away and probably never will.

It was entirely by accident (or was it?)[66] that I had been made aware of the comments sowing the seeds of ill will fabricated to support a case that Steve Graham had gone far enough. I had built an extraordinary practice and had billed more, brought in more, and managed more than most others, some of whom were more highly compensated than I, but now, contrary to evidence and history, my practice was being deemed unsustainable. Every success had to be seen as an aberration. "Just wait," my partners were being warned. "It will happen. Steve Graham will fail. Give it time."

---

66 At all of my firms, I tended to develop a kinship with the staff members and night cleaning crews. As a result, many went out of their way to help me, and on many occasions over the years, secretaries and other staff members would let me know what they heard other partners say about me. Examples include the letter from a client general counsel praising my work brought to me by a secretary and the time a secretary came to warn me about plans being laid to have me fired. My unfiltered partner-compensation notebooks may have been another manifestation of the phenomenon.

The partner compensation committee was being told that, in determining my compensation, they should keep in mind that it would be a challenge to keep me busy. And for good measure, as if being deemed not to have a sustainable practice wasn't enough, let's not forget the latent hostility. I was portrayed as the angry black man, a hostile person who could not be expected to be positive without the intervention of a skilled manager. I am certain that the partner believed that stereotype would sell. If it wasn't for the slipup, I never would have known about this sneak attack. As with so much that goes on behind the scenes, I would have been none the wiser. Just more smiles and more deception.

Eventually, the partner discovered that I had learned what he had said about me. He came to my office and denied everything. I guess he expected me to believe him. I listened. "I didn't say it," he said.

"The comments were too specific for there to be nothing there," I said.

He agreed but insisted that he had been misunderstood. The same, old story: deal with bad facts by denying them. I told him to forget the whole thing.

"I know this will affect our working relationship," he said.

"Don't worry," I replied. "I have not changed my opinion of you."

I terminated the conversation and let him leave. This was the same person, by the way, who would routinely walk in on conversations I was having with other lawyers and interrupt, engaging the other lawyer as if I wasn't there—never asking to be excused, never acknowledging my presence.[67]

---

67 Once, I asked this individual to help me pitch a potential new client. His performance during the pitch was as if he were drunk; it seemed that he was doing his best to ensure that I did not get the work. As it turns out, I was hired, but I never again asked for his assistance.

CHAPTER 17

Black Lives Matter

● ● ●

Too often, African American success is accepted by members of the majority only begrudgingly. Those who find our success difficult to take often lie in wait, anticipating the day when events give them the necessary excuse to reject us and perhaps destroy us. The dean of students at Iowa State University while I was in college was of this mind-set. When we met, he would smile and say all the right things. I believed the smiles to be sincere. They were not.

I sat on campus, waiting in my car for Joanne, my future wife, to come out of Curtiss Hall. It was early evening and there was a slight chill in the air, so I kept the car running. The streets and sidewalks were empty. All was quiet except for the sound of R&B coming over the car stereo. The quiet didn't last. The flashing red lights of a campus police car slowly rolling up behind me changed all that.

My heart rate accelerated. Too often for me, a law enforcement officer signaled trouble. I have lost count of the number of times I have been harassed by the police.[68] In Ames, Iowa, they would sometimes tail me around town, occasionally pulling me over for no particular reason. Once, they followed Joanne and me into her driveway, apparently for sport. They sat behind us for several minutes before backing out and disappearing into the night. In Seattle, a highway patrolman pulled me over (I was driving a silver Mercedes at the time), and the first thing he asked me was whether I was employed. I didn't answer but instead handed him my business card.[69] No other words were spoken. In Chicago one night, police drew their guns on me to intimidate me or perhaps to actually shoot me. I believe that the only thing that saved me that night in an alley behind a South Side apartment building was my college-student ID.

I watched in my rearview mirror as the campus policeman climbed out of his car: white, middle-aged. He stretched a bit and straightened his cap before carefully approaching my car, one hand on his nightstick. I rolled down the window and prepared for another confrontation. The policeman leaned down. He was unsmiling and

---

68 I should add that I have had many positive interactions with law enforcement as well, such as the time a motorcycle cop followed me into a gas station and offered to help me pump my gas before suggesting that in the future, I should avoid running red lights such as the one I had just run in my haste to get to a pump before I ran out of gas. He was then on his way without writing me a ticket. Unfortunately, however, it is the negative experiences that linger and color perceptions.

69 At the time, I didn't think about how dangerous that act of reaching into my coat pocket for a business card could be.

unfriendly. My jaw tightened as I maintained my silence. After a few moments, he spoke. "There is no parking here, young man. You're going to have to move along."

I really wasn't interested in moving from the empty street. I wasn't in anyone's way, and Joanne would be coming out shortly. I sized up the situation, shrugged my shoulders, and took a deep breath. "I am not parking," I replied. "I am standing."

My response caught the policeman by surprise. Momentarily off balance, he quickly regained his footing. He narrowed his eyes. "Don't get smart with me," he snapped. "That sign over there says No Parking. Now move along."

I looked beyond the policeman, read the sign, and checked the classroom building. Still no Joanne. Not time to leave yet. "That's nice," I said. "That is, in fact, what the sign says. But do you know what the sign means?" I paused and then answered the question for him. "Apparently not."

The policeman opened his mouth, but no words came.

I smiled. "I am not parking," I said. "I am standing. There is a difference between parking and standing. I think you should know that." I grinned.

The policeman stiffened. "You had better move along, son, before you find yourself in serious trouble."

I had no intention of moving along. "I don't know why you feel the need to threaten me," I said. "That is not going to help anything." The policeman's face began to redden. "Let me explain," I began. "As you correctly note, that sign says No Parking. You will also note that it says nothing else. There are other similar signs around the campus, however, as you are no doubt aware, that say No Parking, Stopping, or Standing. Obviously, there must be a difference between parking and standing; otherwise, all of the signs would be the same. I am in my car, and the motor is running. That is the definition of standing. Again, that sign says No Parking. I am not parking. I am standing." I smiled at the policeman.

He slammed his hands down on the windowsill and gripped the door of my car, fighting to restrain himself. "Listen, you smart-aleck little..." He didn't finish his sentence but started a new one. "You had better get the hell out of here!" He was shaking now and feeling for his nightstick. His blood pressure was on the rise, and he was looking for something to club—most likely me.

Still no Joanne. But I was starting to feel the heat. Whether my position was right or wrong didn't matter anymore. I had pushed this guy far enough, and it was time to back off. *Lucky for me*, I thought as I began my retreat, *all he has is a nightstick*. With recent police shootings (specifically at Jackson State[70]) and my own Chicago experience

---

70 On May 14, 1970, police fired for about thirty seconds on a group of African American students at Jackson State, the historically black college in Jackson, Mississippi, killing two and wounding eleven others. (I suggest looking at your watch and waiting for thirty seconds to go by.) An FBI investigation revealed that about 400 bullets or pieces of buckshot had been fired into Alexander Hall. www.npr.org/templates/story/story.php?storyId=126426361.

in mind, I alluded to this fortunate bit of foresight on the part of the university's policy makers as I drove away. "It's a good thing they don't allow you guys to carry guns," I called out. "Otherwise, you would have shot me."

A short time later, I circled back to pick up Joanne. I described the incident to her. We laughed and thought that was the end of it—it wasn't.

I soon found myself summoned to the office of the dean of students. The policeman had filed a complaint against me, alleging that I had threatened to kill him. My words had become, "It's a good thing that I don't have a gun. Otherwise, I would shoot you."

The dean of students, who up to that time had been very friendly, turned his back on me in an instant, readily embracing the policeman's narrative. Delighted to be able to confirm that I was just like "the rest of them," the dean accepted as true the white cop's story about the violence-prone, militant black student sporting the outrageous Afro. After all, it fit the stereotype. He treated me with utter loathing and told me that I was going to be expelled. Until that day, I had naïvely believed the dean to be a friend. I saw things more clearly now. He had feigned respect only because he felt he had no other choice. He had never fully embraced the concept of equality and viewed me as an oddity, entitled only to superficial acceptance, to be rejected at the first opportunity. The policeman had given him that opportunity. He couldn't have been happier.

Some sort of trial with a student jury was scheduled. The dean of students, so it seemed, would first convene a kangaroo court, creating the appearance of fairness and thereby legitimizing my lynching, a practice not uncommon on university campuses. Once the "court" found against me, I would be expelled, and with that expulsion, I would lose any chance of getting into a decent law school—or perhaps any law school at all. The dean of students was pleased. He was putting me in my place. There had been no witnesses. It would be the policeman's word against mine. Perfect.

At the "trial," my strategy would be simple: tell the truth. State the facts without emotion and without embellishment, and allow those facts, and their telling, to speak for themselves. It would be the policeman's word against mine, but if the students on the jury were fair minded, that should be enough.

I took the stand and told my story. The students nodded along. Joanne corroborated my version of the facts as best she could. Although she hadn't been an actual witness to the events, she was able to tell the story as I had related it to her at the time.

After we finished, it was the policeman's turn. He took the stand full of misplaced self-importance and overconfidence. He smiled at me as if to say, "I've got you now, you smartass son of a bitch." I listened as he wove his story of the menacing black man who had threatened to kill and who *would* kill if given the chance, drawing upon the stories he had been hearing all of his life. The university had been lucky this time, but would it be so lucky the next? This black threat must be removed before something terrible happens. No one on the campus was safe as long as this man's violence-prone presence was permitted. Do you want to be his victim? How about your loved ones? If not, then you know what you must do.

He was selling bigotry. But the student jury wasn't buying. The jurors frowned at the officer as he told his story. He sensed that they weren't impressed with his version of the facts, so he embellished, making matters worse for himself and further eroding his credibility before an increasingly skeptical group. The dean squirmed, growing uneasy as he watched his instrument of my destruction self-destruct.

At the close of the proceedings, the jurors found in my favor. I would not be expelled and my future would, for the moment, remain on track.

The policeman was dumbfounded. He sat there alone, looking dazed and awkward and unsure of what had just happened. How could this be? Who had tinkered with the script? He was the respectable white authority figure, and I was the lowly African American. I could be lynched at will, for sport. No one would care. Indeed, they would be pleased if he gave them an excuse. He would be a hero. That certainly was the case with the dean. Fortunately for me, though, that was not so with the students. They gathered around me, offering apologies and congratulations.

As Joanne and I prepared to leave the makeshift court-room and put the episode behind us, the policeman made an attempt to cut his losses. He approached and tried to apologize for the "misunderstanding." At the same time, the dean regrouped, reapplied his façade, and sought to renew our "friendship," saying how pleased he was that I had been exonerated. I didn't know whether to laugh or cry. I politely made it very clear to both that I wasn't interested in either of them.

CHAPTER 18

Crossing the Line

● ● ●

THERE HAVE BEEN THOSE OVER the years who have spent a great deal of time and effort trying to discredit me and hold me back for no discernable legitimate reason. I'm speaking less now of unconscious bias and more about open hostility. In these situations, it was as if my mere existence on this planet had triggered in a person some sort of visceral reaction. That certainly is what I confronted in the case of two trucking company acquisitions I handled for Burlington Northern in the small-town South. First, though, I handled an acquisition in Indianapolis. That transaction proved to be as uneventful as it was successful. So it was on to Joplin, Missouri, where I saw the first sign of trouble.

I landed at Joplin's tiny airport and was met by one of the target company's employees, who drove me across town to the all-hands meeting. I was the last to arrive. The other players had already assembled in a spacious conference room, my team occupying one side of the large table and the target company's team the other. Everyone seemed engaged, passing the time with small talk. I took a spot, unloaded my briefcase, and settled in to lead my side of the negotiations. As we prepared to begin, the target company's lawyer stared at me as if to ask, rhetorically, what I was doing there. I glanced up and caught his glare—this was familiar and unpleasant territory for me.[71] Sizing up the competition, I just smiled. His glare intensified. I turned my attention elsewhere.

As the businesspeople began discussing the transaction's terms, I listened, observed, and took notes, adding brief clarifying comments or gently asking questions as we proceeded. At the first major sticking point, I considered the back-and-forth and began to formulate ideas as to how we might resolve the issue presented. The discussion finally stalled, and I moved to propose a solution.

On impulse, the target company's attorney erupted. "No one asked you!" he shouted. "You have no idea what we are trying to accomplish here. You were not privy to the earlier conversations. You are meddling where you

---

71 I cannot recount all of the times over the years when I have found myself in similar situations where I was made to feel, at best, unwelcome. I have grown accustomed to attending meetings and receiving the clear message that, in the opinion of some, I didn't belong. Many times, I have felt the sting of a fellow professional or businessman looking right through me as if I wasn't there, summarily dismissed as someone not worth talking or listening to. Those who did acknowledge my existence would sometimes invite comment out of courtesy but turn their attention elsewhere at the first possible moment, often while I was in midsentence. Others would simply ask, "Why are you here?"

shouldn't be. I suggest that you stay out of this and keep your mouth shut before you jeopardize this deal!"

The attack was direct, extreme, almost violent, and clearly personal. It reminded me of the time in Anchorage, Alaska, when at the end of a few days of negotiations, opposing counsel shouted at me from across the table, "You asshole!" I had done nothing to warrant that attack other than insist that we take the time to run through a closing checklist.[72] My client had turned to me, saying, "I think that was personal."

The Joplin lawyer seemed to have little stomach for African Americans on the playing field, regardless of which side they represented. He seemed to be of the view that white professionals should not be required to interact with African Americans as equals. Indeed, African Americans should not be allowed in the room. My active participation in his deal had caused his head to explode.

Shocked by the Joplin lawyer's irrational outburst, my client looked to me for clues as to how to respond. Did he need to say something? I slowly shook my head. Showing no emotion, I shrugged and settled back in my chair, encouraging everyone to proceed. My client followed my lead.

---

72 When I said that I was going to go over my checklist to make sure everything was in order, opposing counsel exclaimed, "What do you think we have been doing for the past three days?" He then said that he didn't want to spend time on it. I told him that he could do whatever he wanted to do, but that I was going to review my checklist. That's when he yelled the insult.

With me quiet and presumably out of the way, the Joplin lawyer redirected his attention to the businesspeople. I stayed in the background, content to remain invisible for the moment. I could wait. My job was to keep my eye on the ball and get the deal done. I would wait for an opening where I would insert myself into the process. One always came.

The wife of the owner of the target company attended every negotiating session but contributed nothing. She whiled away the hours looking at me and practicing her hate stare, sending the clear signal that she held me in contempt. Each time I entered the room, she ran her eyes up and down me, frowning as if she smelled something bad. She never called me Steve, or Mr. Graham, or anything else that might suggest respect. She only called me "hon." Everybody else, it seemed, received a real name or title. All I got was "hon," and in my case it was not a term of endearment. It was her version of "boy."

As that first day dragged on, questions directed to my client were redirected by my client to me. The client consistently asked me for my views and, after hearing them, would usually agree with me. The Joplin lawyer soon learned that he had no choice but to deal with the African American in the room. In time, albeit with reluctance, he put aside the baggage he had brought to the table and began to show acceptance.

Over the course of the ensuing days, I established my credibility and won the respect of everyone present (except, perhaps, the owner's wife). The Joplin lawyer and I began to approach issues in a collaborative way, developing constructive and practical solutions. Eventually, the transaction was completed successfully, and the two of us parted with feelings of mutual respect. When we had first met, the Joplin lawyer saw only my race, a race defined by stereotypes he had spent a lifetime absorbing. By the time we were finished, he viewed me as an individual. He even invited me to return to Missouri to stay at his home.

Unlike the lawyer and the wife, from the day we met, the owner had treated me as an equal. While much older than I, he embraced me, contrary to what I might have expected based on stereotypes of Southern white men of his generation. Perhaps he had worked the hardest to achieve individual success, understood the struggle, and was secure in his own skin. He had nothing to prove to anybody or anything to fear from anybody. He had spent his life competing against himself, never losing sleep over what someone else had or didn't have, did or didn't deserve. He had no sense of entitlement and believed that if he worked hard, he would be okay. He was confident in his own abilities and did not feel the need to put anyone down in order to give himself meaning. We had a small closing lunch and parted company in mutual respect.

The hostility directed toward me in Joplin had been evident to my client. Indeed, when I wasn't present, the racism was expressed more openly. My client, however, withheld comment. Another critical point not lost on my client was the fact that, through it all, I had handled myself confidently and skillfully, using the other side's misguided attitudes to keep them off balance.

Several days after closing the Joplin deal, my client called to say that the next deal would be in Monroe, Louisiana. Although we had never discussed it and I had never mentioned it, during that call, my client acknowledged Joplin's less-than-progressive social environment and the extreme animosity directed toward me. My client asked whether, under the circumstances, I would be willing to travel to Monroe. It had been hot in Joplin; it would be much hotter in Monroe. My first thought was to decline the invitation, but good opportunities for me were hard to come by, so I acted against my better judgment. "Sure, I will travel to Monroe," I answered, regretting those six words as soon as they were spoken. "No problem," I added without conviction.

"Great!" responded my client.

I hung up the phone, cursing myself. I spent the rest of the day regretting what I now considered a huge mistake.

A few days later, the client called back. The client had had second thoughts. "About the Monroe, deal," the client began. "We really want you do it for us, but given the attitudes we are likely to encounter, we would understand if you would rather not."

I couldn't believe my good fortune. I was being handed a second chance to save myself. I was not about to make the same mistake twice. "Thanks for your understanding," I said. "I appreciate the opportunity, but if the truth be known, I would rather not go."

After a slight pause, the client answered. "Yes, we do understand. We will find someone else."

"Thanks," I said with mixed feelings. The weight rising from my shoulders was palpable, but I also knew that, once again, I was losing out on a rare opportunity due to issues involving race—only this time by my own choosing.

I assumed that was the end of it, but it wasn't. A few days later, the client called back. "We've been thinking. We really want you to do the Monroe deal. What would you do if we insisted that you do it?"

I sighed and slumped in my chair. I was torn. "If you insisted, I would do it," I replied. "I would rather not, but if you really want me to, if you think it is that important, of course I will do it."

"That's great!" he said. "In that case, we insist!"

"Okay, then," I said, trying hard to hide my disappointment. "Let's go get a deal done."

The phone line fell silent momentarily. "We are on, then?" asked the client, in search of confirmation.

"Absolutely," I said, "We're on."

"Great! Details to follow!"

I slowly hung up the phone.

Before the end of the week, the client called back once more. "Hello. Steve?"

Now what? I thought. "Yes," I said.

"We've been doing some more thinking," they said. "We are concerned that we are forcing you to do something that you really don't want to do. If you feel that strongly about not going to Monroe, we will find someone else to do the deal."

A third chance to save myself. "Have you found that someone?" I asked.

"Not yet," was the reply.

I briefly thought about backing out, but by now, I had resigned myself to going. In my own mind, at least, I had crossed the point of no return. "Don't give it another thought," I said. "The discussion is closed. I am your lawyer all of the time, not just when it's convenient."

I had never traveled in northern Louisiana, and I didn't know what to expect. I held certain negative preconceptions, but I hoped for a pleasant surprise. My hope was misplaced.

The Delta 737 touched down in Monroe early one sunny afternoon. My client and I were greeted at the airport by a young man employed by the target company. After a round of handshaking accompanied by welcoming noises, the employee cheerfully ferried us to the office of the target's lawyer.

The office was located in a small, single-story building. The feel of my marble-and-mahogany palace back in Seattle was light-years away from this. The reception-ist ushered the group into a cramped conference room. I found a chair and sat down strategically near the door in an attempt to maximize my access to fresh air. The fake-walnut-veneered conference table proved much too small for the assembled multitude, but it would have to do.

Amid the sounds of creaking chairs and documents and briefcases thudding onto the table, the parties exchanged business cards, confirmed the objectives for the day, re-viewed the deal terms, and discussed logistics. Eventually, we turned our attention to the merger agreement.

The owner of the target was an older gentleman named John Smith. I called him John and continued to do so during the first fifteen minutes of the negotiations. His lawyer, on the other hand, knowing his place and clearly showing a higher level of deference, addressed him only as "Mr. Smith." As the "John/Mr. Smith" contrast continued, I grew increasingly uneasy. I was hypersensitive to the fact that I was not in the most progressive part of the South. The history of the region was long, rich, and varied, but the part that played with my mind was its history of slavery, Jim Crow, and murder of African Americans with impunity.

During the period from Reconstruction through World War II, at least 540 lynchings occurred in Louisiana, placing it third behind Georgia and Mississippi. At least thirty-five of Louisiana's lynchings had been perpetrated in Ouachita Parish, where Monroe is. I did not want to of-fend or to appear to be stepping out of my place any more than I had already simply by showing up and taking a seat at the table. Any avoidable distractions resulting from any perceived offense on my part could jeopardize the deal, not to mention my own well-being. I stopped the negotiations and turned to Mr. Smith.

"Excuse me, sir," I said. "I keep calling you 'John,' while your lawyer keeps calling you 'Mr. Smith.' How should I address you? As 'John' or as 'Mr. Smith?'"

The gentleman leaned back in his chair, looked me in the eye, cast a glance over at his lawyer, and then turned back to me. With his slow drawl, he said, smiling, "Well, son, mah name is 'John.'"

Mr. Smith seemed pretty happy with himself. Clearly, he wasn't interested in putting me down. In fact, he had elevated me a notch or two above his own lawyer, whom we will call Jones. Jones was clearly taken aback by the arrangement. He forced a smile, but as he shot a glance my way, there was no mistaking the hate simmering behind his eyes. The tension in the room began its slow upward climb.

The rules of engagement thus established, we restarted the negotiations, with me and Jones addressing the owner in our different ways. Predictably, as the negotiations wore on, Jones grew increasingly hostile. He made it clear to me that he did not like Yankees, he did not like Ivy League lawyers, he did not like big law firms, and he sure as hell didn't have time for black people, the latter point being expressed somewhat more obliquely than the others. As we worked our way through the merger agreement, Jones went from a simmer to a boil. I caught him staring at me as if I were in a zoo and imagined that he must be imagining a rope, a tree, and me.

The meeting dragged on well into the evening. By the time we called it quits, my client had achieved his initial objectives and was satisfied. We discussed next steps, reloaded our briefcases, and said our good-byes. I would be returning to Seattle in the morning. Another trip to Monroe would be required to wrap up negotiations and to prepare and execute final documents.

The idea of returning to Monroe did not sit well with me. I actually feared for my life. This was perhaps the product of an overactive imagination, but nevertheless, it was my reality, and I couldn't convince myself otherwise. Indeed, my instincts, which were usually spot-on, urged me not to return under any circumstances.

In the days that followed, although safe in Seattle, I was haunted by a deep sense of foreboding. I wanted out. The mere thought of getting on a plane headed for Monroe kept me up at night. Like it or not, though, a return trip seemed to be in my future. That said, there was no requirement for me to return unarmed. I would bring someone along to watch my back: Dean Freed.

Dean Freed was a great junior corporate finance associate. Not only did we work on deals together, but we regularly played noon pickup basketball games at the Washington Athletic Club, so we were fairly close. He was tall and strong, and he cared about my well-being.

He was also white. Dean riding shotgun was not a bulletproof solution, but it was a reasonable approach likely to be sufficient.

On the night I actually headed to the airport for my flight back to Monroe, the old anxiety returned. Arriving at the airport, I paid the driver, collected my belongings, and slowly pulled myself out of the taxi. Rain was pouring down. The night was black. I felt disconnected from reality, as if in a dream. I wandered inside the terminal, went through security, found my waiting area, and took a seat. The clock struck 11:00 p.m. Any sane person would be home in bed at that hour. At that moment, I didn't think of myself as sane.

In time, the gate agent called for first class. I rose from my seat and headed down the Jetway to the waiting Dallas-bound American Airlines 727. From Dallas, we would fly to Shreveport, and from there on to Monroe. We were scheduled to return home on the 6:00 a.m. flight two days later, twenty-nine hours after leaving Seattle. That gave us about twenty hours to complete the negotiations, redraft and finalize the documents, execute the signature pages, and get the hell out of Monroe. It was going to be tight.

Taking my seat, I settled in and waited for Dean. I gave my drink order—scotch, neat. I downed it quickly in a futile attempt to settle my nerves. Passengers streamed onto the plane and filed past me. In an attempt to ease my mind, I told myself that at least I would have Dean with me, but at that moment, he was nowhere in sight.

In time, the stream of passengers slowed to a trickle—still no Dean. My heart beat a little faster at the prospect of Dean missing the flight. Soon, everyone was seated, and the last few seatbelts were clicking. The flight attendants were making their final preparations. No Dean. I imagined myself bolting from the plane while there was still time. But of course, I held back, not wanting to make a complete fool of myself.

Finally, at the last possible moment, Dean burst through the door with his arms wrapped firmly around a large, black briefcase bulging with paper. I calmly looked up at him and slowly shook my head, concealing my extreme relief. "The taxi broke down," said Dean in explanation as he settled in, trying to catch his breath.

Moments later, the aircraft door slammed shut. Preflight announcements were made as a tractor pushed the plane away from the gate and out onto the tarmac. Soon we were screaming through the darkness, down the wet runway. As we lifted off into the night, I thought, *Well, this is it. There really is no turning back now.* If I had known what lay ahead, there is no way I would have been on that plane.

After spending the night mostly in the air, we touched down in Monroe. It was about 8:00 a.m., local time. We were dog tired, but our work was just beginning.

A car picked us up from our motel for the ride to opposing counsel's office. Once there, insincere pleasantries were exchanged as we prepared to get down to business.

Jones had his pseudo charm back, playing the role of the Southern gentleman but fooling no one. Still, he had dialed back the venom, and for that I was grateful. I relaxed a bit. Perhaps I had in fact allowed my imagination to run wild.

Everyone assumed their old places in the cramped conference room (well, Dean squeezed in next to me), and the negotiations recommenced. I picked up where I had left off with John Smith, as did Jones, each of us addressing him differently. Jones couldn't hide his annoyance, though he seemed to be trying hard. Mr. Smith, for his part, continued to look pleased.

Unfortunately, the day progressed about the way I had predicted. Jones's civilized veneer, as fake as the walnut on the conference table, soon began to peel away. I ignored his snide comments and pointed jabs expressing astonishment at my apparent ability to think. He never missed an opportunity for a derogatory remark, interspersing cracks about Yankees and basketball players, turning my self-deprecating comments against me.

We worked steadily through the day, with me keeping everyone on task—I had a plane to catch, and I had no intention of missing it. Toward the end of the afternoon, we resolved the last few issues, agreed to the language changes, and prepared for closing. At about 5:00 p.m., everything was done except changes to the documents necessary to reflect the final terms.

Jones stretched and said, "Well, that's enough for one day." Dean and I looked at each other knowingly and then in unison turned our eyes to Jones. "Let's all go out and get some dinner," he said, leaning back from the conference table. "We can then go our separate ways, get some rest, and come back in the morning to wrap everything up."

Dean and I again looked at each other. Who was going to tell him?

I was exhausted, having been up now for more than thirty hours. My eyes burned and I felt like hell, but it was not time to stop. Rightly or wrongly, I still perceived a pressing need to leave town as quickly as possible. I felt that my personal safety hung in the balance. "We can break for dinner," I finally announced, "but after dinner, we are coming back to revise and finalize the documents."

Jones dismissed my suggestion. "Sorry," he smirked. "My people go home at five. We all have other plans for tonight."

I countered, saying, "Not tonight. We have already made the arrangements. Your staff is prepared to stay as late as necessary to get all the documents redrafted and photocopied."

The smile dropped from Jones's face. "We will need all of them," he warned.

"I know," I said. "They are all staying." I had managed to engineer a temporary takeover of Jones's office.

He was furious. "No way!" he exclaimed.

"I'm afraid so," I said.

Jones stared at me in bitter silence. Frowning, he turned to his client. He would deal with his employees and their treason later, but for now, he looked to Mr. Smith to shift the tide back in his favor. "Mr. Smith, do you want to come back after dinner and stay late, or just finish up in the morning? I imagine you're pretty tired."

John Smith looked at me with a twinkle in his eye and softly chuckled. He could have been envisioning the millions of dollars that soon would be pouring into his bank account; he needed only to have the documents signed. He also knew that until they were, there was a chance that the deal would never be completed. He slowly rocked and swiveled in his chair, smiling silently, keeping the room in suspense. Finally, he answered. "The sooner we get this deal signed up, the better," he said. "Working late would suit me just fine."

So it was settled. The group would return after dinner to work into the night.

Jones was beside himself. Once again, he held the losing hand. Once again, I had outmaneuvered him. Once again, as far as he was concerned, I had crossed the line. But there was nothing he could do about it. He made no attempt to conceal his disgust, casting a pall over the group.

Without camaraderie, six of us (I, my client, Jones, Dean, and two target-company employees—Mr. Smith had gone home to eat) set off for dinner at a modest restaurant nearby. We took a table on the deck and quietly settled in. Somberly, we ordered our dinners but otherwise maintained our relative silence.

As we were being served, the pressure on Jones to maintain some degree of civility became too great. Without Mr. Smith to serve as a check on his behavior, he began attacking everything and everyone from Democrats to gays, from Catholics to Chinese, from Mexicans to liberals. Inevitably, he turned to African Americans. My face grew hot, but I deflected the words, refusing provocation. Dean stirred in his seat, clearly uneasy. Jones redirected his attack toward Mormons. This time, I took the bait and sided with the Mormons. That proved to be a mistake.

"I used to wonder, too," I said in an attempt to trigger some form of civilized discussion, "but it is clear that their views have become more progressive over the years. People live and learn. I mean, they admitted the error of their teachings and now urge that black people be treated as equals."

Jones looked across the table at me and snickered. I had supplied the opening he had been looking for. "Yes," he sneered, "I used to think a lot of those guys before they did that!" He pounded the table with his fork. "Ha!" he blurted, full of self-satisfaction, proud of his retort. With that, the last of the veneer peeled free, and Jones ended all pretense that he did not despise the ground I walked on. His bigoted remark had everyone staring into their plates in a futile attempt to find cover. We waited for the storm to pass. Unfortunately, it was just beginning.

Jones glared at me with hateful eyes. I tried to ignore him, but it was impossible. In an effort to break the tension, I and the others took turns attempting small talk, each time failing to ignite conversation. Finally, Jones zeroed in. With a flourish, he wiped his hands with his napkin and threw it on the table. He fixed his eyes on me and shattered the still night air along with any lingering semblance of decency. "Wouldn't it be funny," he said, eyes cold and narrow, "if we saw something movin' around in the dark out there and we shot it, and it was you? We would say, 'Oops, we shot Staaave.'"

He watched me, very pleased with himself. He was in his element, sending the clear and potentially terrifying message to an uppity nigger that it might be time for a lynching. What do we do with uppity niggers? We shoot them. It was easier in the old days, but we can still get you.

He waited for my reaction. None came, but, contrary to outward appearances, I was stunned to the core. I swallowed my food with some effort, trying desperately to appear nonchalant. Now what? I was deep in enemy territory, with no means of immediate escape.

Jones took another swipe. "We would say, 'Oops, we shot Staaave.'" He forced a sick little chuckle.

The others stirred uncomfortably. *This is it*, I thought. *This is when I disappear, only to have my body recovered later in some Godforsaken place.* I fought to keep my fear in check and my thinking straight. The level of animosity had risen to the point where bodily harm was becoming a real possibility. My instincts had been correct. I felt simultaneously brilliant and stupid—brilliant for bringing along Dean, stupid for returning in the first place. Now I wondered whether Dean would be enough.

Jones enjoyed his little game, the game of taunting, threatening, and lording it over a black man, making him sweat and fear for his life. Insanely, he kept repeating his little joke. "Wouldn't it be funny if we saw something standing outside the motel and we shot it, and it was you? Ha! We would say, 'Oops, we shot Staaave.'"

There was no brushing aside the seriousness of the attack. It had not been casual but personal and prolonged. My fears no longer seemed irrational. Outwardly, I remained calm while my mind raced through various unpleasant scenarios. How would I respond to any attack that went beyond words? I felt sick to my stomach. My 6:00 a.m. flight was only eleven hours away, but suddenly, that seemed like an eternity.

We finished dinner and drove back to Jones's office in silence. With a renewed sense of urgency, Dean and I threw ourselves headlong into the task of completing the transaction. We pushed ourselves and everyone else to the limit, nearly destroying Jones's modest photocopier, forcing it to churn out hundreds of pages without pause. Jones's staff had seldom, if ever, worked so hard, and they seemed to be having a good time. By 3:00 a.m., the dust had settled, and all the jobs were finished. The conference room table was layered with documents neatly organized, executed, and copied. Mr. Smith was pleased. I was pleased. My client was pleased. Dean was pleased.

Jones was not pleased. He had lost an important client, as his client had been acquired by my client. He had lost most of the battles in his war with a black man he had been forced to accept as his equal, if not his superior. His world was seriously out of alignment, and the only counter he could contemplate was violence, an alternative no longer readily available. Gone were the days when lynching a black man for bumping into a white man on the sidewalk or for looking at a white woman—or for no reason at all— had been commonplace.

The group said their good-byes. Mr. Smith showed a particular fondness for me. We wished each other well and set out into the night.

One of Smith's employees volunteered to drive Dean and me to our small motel out in the middle of nowhere. After the taunts conjuring my shooting, I continued to be on edge. The night was black, and there was plenty of opportunity for a detour and an ambush. I did not want to think about the outcome of the evening if Dean had not been along to serve as some semblance of a check. I didn't want to think about the outcome that was still possible.

In time, we made it safely to the motel and explained to the night clerk that we would be checking out in an hour or so: just enough time to nap, shower, and change before the flight back to Seattle.

I stumbled into my room, exhausted to the breaking point, having had no sleep for nearly two days while being forced to expend emotional and mental energy at levels seldom required of anyone in a routine corporate transaction. All I wanted to do was sleep. But now was not the time to drop my guard. I surveyed the room and considered my defenses. I left the lights off and sat alone in the dark, thinking about unpleasant possibilities. Ground floor. Big windows. Thin doors. Two outside walls. Hardly secure. Had I been placed in this room by design? I sat and I listened. Fighting exhaustion, I struggled to stay awake. I went into the bathroom and in the dark, threw cold water on my face.

A little more awake, I stood in the middle of my room, thinking and listening. A sound caught my ear, and my heart skipped a beat. A car engine had broken the night's stillness. Suddenly, I was on full alert. I listened hard, my heart pounding as the car slowly rolled across the gravel. The crunching and popping seemed to go on forever. Time stood still. I stared into the darkness, concentrating on the sound of the slowly moving car. I had stopped breathing. I waited for the crash of broken glass, the flash of shotgun fire, the shattering of my life, the refrain, "Ooops! We shot Staaave!" reverberating in my head. The popping gravel stopped.

Quietly, I lay flat on the floor. Car doors opened and closed. I heard muffled voices and footsteps on the gravel, then silence. Seconds passed. I pressed my body against the floor. My heart climbed into my throat. More footsteps.

More muffled voices. I could have sworn I heard my name mentioned more than once. Probably just my imagination. I waited. The minutes ticked by. I knew that it was just a matter of time before the windows would shatter or the doors would come crashing down, but the doors and windows remained intact. There were more footsteps. They seemed to be moving away. Car doors opened and closed. Silence. Were they gone? I lay there, alone in the dark, afraid to move, my heart thumping against the floor.

I didn't move until the first light of day began to streak across the horizon. I stood up, looking and feeling disheveled. It was time to make my escape. I used the hotel phone to summon a taxi and to tell Dean to meet me in the motel office. We checked out without incident, pulled our weary bodies into the taxi, and headed in the direction of the airport. We were almost home. It wouldn't be long now.

I watched the taxi driver with suspicion. The highway was lined with thick woods silhouetted against a brightening sky. I imagined the evil that those woods had concealed over the years and wondered what evil the future held for them.

Ultimately, we reached the airport. As we checked in, I began to breathe a little easier. Not until I was walking across the tarmac to the waiting 737, however, did I start to feel safe. Upon reaching my first-class seat, I collapsed and ordered a double scotch. As the aircraft rumbled down the runway and lifted off, I told myself that I would never return to Monroe.

Several days later, my client called. "We would like for you to do another deal for us."

"Sure," I said. "Where to this time?"

"Albany, Georgia."

I didn't have to think twice. "No," I said.

"No?"

Under no circumstances would I be amending my response. "Yes, I said no. I will not be going to Albany, Georgia."

The client found someone else.

CHAPTER 19

The New Jim Crow

● ● ●

AT SOME LEVEL, I CAN accept the bias manifested by those who have not wanted to hire me as their lawyer for the wrong reasons. I would prefer the absence of bias, but at the end of the day, the attorney-client relationship is personal, and the client must feel comfortable with the individual standing by his or her side serving as a trusted advisor. If someone's bias drives her away from African Americans, so be it.

What I cannot accept, however, are those who work to undermine professional relationships having little to do with them, committing the corporate equivalent of hate crimes by going out of their way to cause harm to African Americans. Such was the case with the chief executive officer of Atlas Corporation (not the company's real name). I did not represent him; neither did I seek to. My client was Atlas's investment bank. The CEO nonetheless targeted me for gratuitous harm and aggressively worked to sabotage my business relationship with my client and rob me of an opportunity. He succeeded.

As the meeting to organize the anticipated financing transaction broke up and everyone prepared to leave, I thought it would be good politics for me to give my regards to the Atlas CEO. I approached him. We had not exchanged any words during the meeting, and we had never met prior to that day. "It was nice to meet you," I said, extending my hand. "I look forward to working together." It's just what you said, regardless of whether you meant it. And in polite business circles, the person you are greeting is expected to reply in kind. It's the ritual. I was about to find out, however, that I was not operating in a polite business circle that day.

The Atlas CEO responded to my overture with a sneer as he grudgingly extended his hand. He was a tall, pudgy, middle-aged white man with glasses through which peered unsmiling eyes. Clearly, he was not accustomed to associating with a black man as his relative equal. My diplomatic outreach was brushed aside. Expressing condescension, he asked simply, "Where did you play basketball?" The remark was jarring and pregnant with possibilities, none of them positive.

I considered a number of responses, none of them professional. I chose diplomacy. "I never played basketball," I replied evenly, with a slight smile. I knew my eyes weren't smiling either, and I didn't much care. If the CEO didn't know before, he knew now that the black man standing before him had no intention of operating as anything other than his equal. The tension spiked. His eyes narrowed, and I sensed that we were heading down a path not likely to lead to anything good. I throttled back in an attempt to de-escalate the situation, quickly adding a self-deprecating aside: "I didn't have the skill."

The CEO had no interest in de-escalation. His only interest was putting an African American man in his place, or at least as close to that as was legally possible. "Well," he replied, winding up for another cheap shot, "It's a good thing you decided to become a lawyer. Being a lawyer doesn't require any skill." He pursed his lips and assumed an expression that seemed to say, "Now get out of my face, you uppity little nigger."

I fixed my eyes on his and just smiled. I said nothing more and walked away.

During the drive back to the office, I discussed the incident with the associate who had accompanied me. He was white. He volunteered that he had been shocked and offended by the exchange and asked how I felt. I told him that I had grown accustomed to the almost daily indignities of that nature and tried not to let it bother me. He said that he had no idea that that sort of thinking on the part of a top executive in a Seattle company even existed, let alone would be expressed openly, and that he was not sure if he would have believed it if he hadn't witnessed it for himself. I just welcomed him to my world.

I thought that was pretty much the end of it—but the CEO wasn't finished. He called my client and demanded that I be taken off the deal, that I be fired. After our very brief encounter, he was now going out of his way to use his influence to destroy my opportunity, to push me off the playing field. I was not representing his company; I was representing the investment bank—but he wanted me out of the room. The fact that I occupied a position normally reserved for a white man had pushed his world out of alignment.

There wasn't much he could do to make me lose my position in the whole scheme of things. It was too late for that. I had my Yale degree and my law firm partnership; he couldn't take any of that away. But he certainly could use his power to ensure that he wouldn't have to associate with me and to limit my success to the fullest extent available to him. The far-reaching effects of the attitude exemplified by this particular CEO, coupled with everpresent unconscious bias, have made broad and durable African American success in corporate America as elusive as it is.

My client, anxious to preserve its relationship with the CEO, called my partner who headed our securities group. "Is there another partner you can put on this deal?" he asked. "The CEO doesn't want Graham."

Behind the scenes; in the shadows: there is no way of knowing how many times throughout my career similar conversations have taken place. Someone suggests me for an opportunity, and the opportunity responds by saying, directly or obliquely, "Is there someone other than the African American?" And with eyes firmly fixed on self-interest, the someone recommends an attorney of a lighter shade. This is why it can be so difficult for minority professionals to progress and why it can be so difficult to determine precisely why. There is so much that operates beneath the surface—things just happen. Things don't go our way, and we are left to wonder why, all the while receiving assurances that we are supported, that the deck is not stacked, and that everyone is committed to equal opportunity. Occasionally, however, as in this instance, the efforts to undermine are exposed.

"Why?" asked my colleague. "What's wrong with Graham?"

"Bad vibes," was the reply. A familiar story. Bad vibes. Not a good fit. Won't play well. Send the African American down the path of limited opportunity, and then feign puzzlement[73] when his career is stunted, failing to acknowledge or even appreciate that the cause may be the cumulative effect of these seemingly small slights.

"So," continued the head of our group, "after a two-minute interchange, he got bad vibes? Seems odd. And why does it matter, anyway, since Graham is representing you and not him? Why not wait to go through a drafting session or two so as to at least lend some credibility to his conclusions?"

"Can't do that," said the banker. Obviously, the CEO was putting pressure on the bank. The banker was a white

---

73 Admittedly, some who engage in behavior having a broad negative impact on minorities are sufficiently clueless that they honestly cannot understand why minorities may be struggling.

man, and he had to have known what was happening, but at a minimum, he cared more about profit and short-term goals than diversity and fairness, two ideas apparently worth his consideration only when convenient, if at all.

The situation was discussed among a few of my group's partners. I was unaware of the behind-the-scenes shenanigans at that point and thus was not a party to these discussions. Following them, however, I was made aware, and my opinion was solicited. I expressed my disappointment in the racist attitudes, but I said I didn't care—that it was fine with me if the firm still took on the transaction but I didn't do the work myself.[74] Within limits, it is best to accept reality and move on.

My partners, however, were troubled. For them, in this instance, a line had been crossed. They concluded that it was too likely that the coded messages ("fit," "vibes," and all the rest) were evidence of blatant racism if not outright bigotry. The firm would disassociate itself from actions subject to this ready interpretation. The client was called back. "If we do the work, Graham will handle it. If you want someone else, you will have to go to another firm."

We didn't do the deal.

---

74 At times, in similar situations, I have taken the position that it did not matter to me if my firm took on a certain client even in the wake of suspicious behavior, because often you just don't know. It will become a judgment call that a partner will have to make for himself. In anticipation of the fee, the potential client is often given the benefit of the doubt. In the Atlas situation, however, there could be little doubt as to what was going on.

CHAPTER 20

What's Yours Is Mine

● ● ●

RELATIVE TO THE OPPORTUNITIES AFFORDED white males in corporate America, the opportunities for African Americans are few. Adding insult to injury, it is not unusual for opportunities once obtained by African Americans to be taken from them.

One of my Yale professors suggested that I identify a state, move there, and become its governor. In terms of leadership positions, however, my first firm initially held a much less lofty view of my talents. Early in my career, I asked to be placed on firm committees but was always rejected.[75] Ultimately, as I often did, I decided to take matters into my own hands.

I approached the chair of the hiring committee and expressed concern about the continued absence of minority lawyers at the firm. Not wanting to blame the firm,

---

75 As a junior partner, I did serve a short stint on the hiring committee, but the group, as composed, was deemed too radical and was quickly disbanded. In time, I served on the executive committee and the partner compensation committee.

I blamed the city. I argued that while the firm was well meaning and receptive, Seattle was not a big enough draw for minority law students. Expressing certainty that the firm shared my goal of increasing diversity among its lawyers, I argued that it needed to educate law students about the opportunities available in Seattle in general and at the firm in particular. The chair was receptive and asked me to formulate a plan. The minority-hiring task force was born.

I assembled a group of interested lawyers, and we developed a program designed to attract minority law students to the area, drawing in other Seattle law firms to collaborate. At the core of the program was a series of receptions at selected law schools to be conducted over a two- or three-year period, scheduled in advance of the regular fall on-campus interviews.

Under my leadership, the program flourished—then it happened. I was called into a meeting with the managing partner, the then-chair of the hiring committee,[76] and two representatives of the task force. I didn't know it at the time, but the meeting was part of a plan to take the task force from me. During the meeting, it was first offered as a suggestion, and then, when I resisted, offered as an accomplished fact, that the task force would be rolled into the hiring committee. Since the task force was a part of the hiring program, so went the reasoning, it made no

---

76 The partner who had helped and supported me in this effort had by this time passed away.

sense to keep it separate. Furthermore, since it just so happened that I was not on the hiring committee, someone else would have to take over leadership of the firm's efforts to attract minority lawyers. Placing me on the hiring committee apparently was not viewed as a viable option.

I started to argue but was summarily cut off. No one was interested in my point of view. No one in the room came to my support. I realized that the meeting's conclusions had been prearranged without the courtesy of any advance discussion with me. My leadership role in minority hiring was to be terminated. The significant administrative role that I had carved out for myself was being taken away. Someone didn't want me leading anything of significance on behalf of the firm, not even the committee I had created. Everyone in the room was in on the joke except me. My only question was why they even bothered to hold the meeting.

Once, while an associate, I had handled all the negotiations and document drafting for a client in connection with an important financing. There was nothing left to do except attend and manage the formal closing in New York City. I spent the last day reviewing the closing details with the client in my office. He didn't seem to care much for me, which I dismissed as nothing new. When the client left my office that evening, I told him that I would see him in New York. He nodded in agreement and gave me a thin smile. That smile said everything—only I wasn't paying attention.

Later that evening, I got a call at home. It was the partner on the deal. "Steve, I'm calling to let you know that we are going to send another associate to New York to handle the closing instead of you." We will call that other associate Robert.

My stomach did a double take, and I felt slightly nauseous. I really didn't need this. "I'm not understanding," I said in disbelief. "What's going on here?"

"Well, the client called, and he said he would feel more comfortable with Robert."

"More comfortable?" I queried. "And that is code for what, exactly?"

"It's not code for anything. He just thinks that Robert would be a better fit."

"You're not making any sense," I said. "And it's my deal."

"Not anymore," said the partner. "Sorry. I know the client is being irrational, but he pays the bills. He gets to have his way."

"Did you push back?" I asked.

"What? What do you mean?" asked the partner.

"Did you defend me, or did you just roll over?"

The partner did not respond immediately.

"Well?" I prodded.

"I told him I disagreed," said the partner.

"But did you push back?" I asked. "Did you really argue on my behalf like I would have argued on my behalf?"

Silence.

"You didn't, did you?" I said. "In the end, you were satisfied with the results, so the hell with me."

Silence.

"Why are you letting this happen? What's really going on? Why don't you have my back?"

"I do have your back," said the partner. "I know that all the documents are drafted, all the issues are put to bed, and everything is pretty much set, but things always come up at the last minute, and the client feels that you don't have the experience to handle any surprises—at least not in the way Robert does."

"That's fucking bullshit," I said into the phone, trying and failing to remain calm. "And you know it! Objectively, I have more experience than Robert, especially in these matters!"

The partner ignored my point. He just went on, "And Robert knows the client and wants to go."

"Wants to go!" I yelled, unable to contain myself any longer. "What's that got to do with anything? My God!"

"Well," the partner said in an effort to conclude the matter, clearly uneasy, "if you must know, the client said that you wouldn't play well in New York."

"What the hell!" I said. "What is *that* supposed to mean?"

Clearly, the partner had let something slip that had not been intended for my ears. He stammered but could offer little by way of justification. Obviously, he was merely the messenger, and he was doing a very poor job of it. Someone would rather have an associate who knew nothing about the transaction represent the company in New York than me, because that other associate would "play" better. The client hadn't had the spine to tell that to me. The partner hadn't had the spine to come to my defense.

"I should go," I said. "I am the one who put this deal together. This is ridiculous. The only thing left to do is to close it. You know it would be unfair to pull me at this point. You can't do this. You have no valid reason." I continued on with arguments in my defense.

There was nothing legitimate that the partner could say in response. There was only one correct answer. We both knew that racism was at work here but chose to ignore the elephant in the room. "This isn't going very well," the partner said.

"No, it isn't!" I agreed.

The partner stammered around without clear direction, approaching incoherency. In the end, the phone line fell silent.

Your move, I thought. *I'm not helping you out of this.* Silence.

Finally, the partner spoke. "As usual, you have been very persuasive," he said. "You should go."

"You're damn right, I should go!" I shouted.

"Why don't you plan on going?" said the partner. "I'll talk to Robert." The partner signed off, and the phone fell silent one last time.

The evening's unwelcome interlude was at an end. I experienced a brief moment of triumph before spiraling into a state of depression. Why did I have to fight for every inch? Why was it that the ice under me never thickened? I went to bed, feeling like quitting.

The next morning, I walked into an ambush. Shortly after I arrived at the office, the partner pulled me aside. He looked like hell. "You are not going to New York," he said with conviction, clearly not inviting a response. "Give Robert what he needs to close the deal. You will not be traveling to New York on behalf of the company. That's final."

I started to say something. I was summarily cut off.

"There is nothing to talk about," said the partner. "I'm sorry." He turned and walked away, throwing up his hands.

So Robert, who had nothing to do with the transaction, flew off to further his career while I stayed behind. For me, another missed opportunity.

On the morning of the closing, I confirmed the filing of one of the documents that our firm's legal opinion hinged upon. I called New York to let Robert know that he could release the opinion. I got the New York lawyer. "Thank you for your call," was the reply, "but we're done. Your firm's opinion was delivered some time ago. We've closed the deal, and everyone's gone. I appreciate, though, your professionalism."

Robert had delivered our opinion in a financing involving tens of millions of dollars before receiving confirmation that everything was in place. But I guess the details weren't important. The important thing was that Robert was in New York representing the client, and not me.

When the firm sought the work of the Hongkong and Shanghai Banking Corporation, I participated in the early office discussions but was excluded from the ultimate lunch with the potential client. We eventually landed the work, and Chris Bailey became the billing lawyer—i.e., the lawyer who received primary credit for revenue generated by the client, a very important component of partner compensation. I helped with the work whenever called upon and developed a strong relationship with the bank.

A few years later, when Chris decided to leave the firm, he took the position that billing responsibility should be transferred to me, ensuring that I would receive that statistical credit in the partner compensation process. It was not a popular position in some circles. Some argued that it would be inappropriate to make me the billing lawyer. A more senior lawyer was required, went the argument. This was just another way of saying that the client should be passed down to a white guy, not the black guy. Chris argued against them on the merits. I was the logical successor; I had done all the work. I had built the relationship.[77] In the end, Chris prevailed, much to the displeasure of two

---

[77] During one transaction involving the bank, its officers asked for my advice regarding a strategic move. I outlined the various scenarios and laid out the options. They listened and then asked me what I would do. I told them that it was a business decision and they had to decide. So they called New York for guidance. New York told them to "do whatever Steve Graham thinks best." Ultimately, I made the call.

other individuals who had tried to seize the opportunity, and I took over management of the account.[78]

Several years later, I lost the client anyway because the managing partner decided that in the face of a conflict, the firm would rather represent a bankrupt clothing company that owed the bank money than one of the most powerful financial institutions in the world. It was a bad business decision, but I suppose it served the managing partner's purposes.

---

78 It is rare in the law-firm context to see significant clients passed down to women and minorities. This fact helps to depress the compensation of women and minorities. It also encourages them to leave their firms.

CHAPTER 21

If You Can't Beat Him, Discredit Him

● ● ●

THE ABSENCE OF AFRICAN AMERICANS at prominent law firms, corporations, accounting firms, and investment banks has been a continuing source of concern for me. In my own small way, through mentoring, recruiting, and promoting awareness, I have tried to do something about it, unashamedly favoring African American associates those times when opportunity allocation was within my power.

While with Perkins, I decided to attend a minority-law-student job fair in Atlanta as part of an effort to widen our minority-recruiting net. The event drew students attending law schools all over the southern region of the United States, schools that, primarily due to geography, we would never tap into from Seattle. I submitted our baseline hiring criteria to those running the event and, eventually, I received a report back that ten or twelve students had signed up to interview with me. I flew from Seattle to Atlanta with high expectations, assuming that I had gained access to a significant pool of highly qualified minority law students previously unavailable to us. Unfortunately, the trip that had begun with such promise ended in disappointment and frustration. Contrary to what had been represented, none of the students who signed up met our baseline criteria. The whole trip proved to be a gigantic waste of time for me and, frankly, for the students, who must somehow have been misled.

Shortly after returning from Atlanta, I was contacted by a *Seattle Times* reporter doing an article on minority hiring in law firms. Among other things, we discussed my recent experience in Atlanta and the minority job fair sponsored by the University of Washington drawing minority law students from the western region of the United States. In the article that eventually appeared in the newspaper, I was quoted out of context to make it appear that I believed that no student attending any minority job fair anywhere would qualify for positions at our firm—when my actual reference was regarding the specific students I had seen in Atlanta.

Certain partners at Perkins were quick to believe what the paper had insinuated regarding my opinion of minority students resorting to job fairs in search of employment. They immediately condemned me for expressing a view that I had not expressed. They believed that by saying what I did not say, I had placed the firm in a negative light. (It gets confusing when you assume things and play fast and loose with the facts. But once again, the facts were of little concern.) These partners believed what they wanted to believe. They believed what best fit their preconceived notions or otherwise furthered their agenda. The public expression of my alleged view was taken as concrete proof of my incompetence, lack of common sense, and poor judgment, even though the underlying "fact" was essentially a fabrication. My colleagues took the suggestions of the reporter at face value and, having conjured their evidence of weapons of mass destruction, launched their attack on me for single-handedly ruining the firm's reputation.

No one bothered to ask me about the situation. Apparently, my side of the story could be determined without any input from me. As lawyers, they should have known better—but, of course, as lawyers, they did. The truth, however, had no role in this game; other objectives were at play. It seems that some were upset by the mere fact that the *Seattle Times* had called me and that my public profile was being further raised.

I called the newspaper reporter and asked him what the hell was going on, something the firm hadn't bothered to do. His response was that he had intentionally written the article in a misleading way to provoke controversy. He was of the view that students who attended minority job fairs were subpar and unqualified for associate positions at big law firms, but he couldn't find anyone to say that, so he had made it appear as if I had. If any of my detractors were interested in the truth, or at least engaging in minimal fact gathering before proceeding with their collective condemnation, they could have made the same call and discovered what I had.

I was slammed with a barrage of e-mails and voicemails critical of my behavior and taking me to task for something I had not done. A feeding frenzy erupted, accompanied by an intense competition to see who could throw me under the bus first. No one—not one person—came to my support, a stark reminder of how alone I stood. I was back on that Iowa playground with some white kid screaming in my face, "Go to hell, nigger!" and reminding me that, notwithstanding the thin veneer of civility that sugarcoated most days, I was different from the majority, and too many chose to see that difference in a negative light.

The incident later surfaced as a mark against me in the partner compensation process. I was rebuked as follows: "Moreover, there have been a few other occasions in which your administrative judgment has been questioned. Examples include...the newspaper flap over minority recruiting."

Amazing, really, the extent to which some would go to find fault, seizing upon lies to support their findings if that's all there was. I responded:

In the area of community involvement, I was criticized because of what was described as "the newspaper flap over minority recruiting." This criticism is unfair. As one of the very few minority lawyers in a major law firm in Seattle, indeed, the country, I believe that it is appropriate for me to speak to the issues relating to minority participation in the legal profession, and to provide some leadership in this area, both within the firm and within the community, if not the country. Prior to the "flap" I publicly spoke on these issues, on television and otherwise, contributing to the firm's positive image as a result. I will continue to speak on these issues. It is unfortunate that a quote in the newspaper, taken out of context, led to the suggestion that I believed that most students participating in minority job fairs would not meet our standards, but I have little control over the press.

What happened next? Nothing. No apology. Nothing. Knives were simply resheathed as Brutus and the boys retreated back into the shadows to await the next opportunity.

In another attempt at character assassination, as part of the partner compensation process, it was reported that I lacked good judgment because I had tried to use firm frequent-flyer coupons for personal flights. This was something I had never done. The lie was accepted, made a part of the record, and used against me. Again, no one asked me about it. They had heard someone else's side of the story and, with no diligence, accepted it as true. I countered:

In the area of cost-effective operation and administrative judgment, last year I was criticized for "a request to use Alaska Airlines coupons for personal travel." This was the first I had ever even heard of the existence of such coupons. This is not true and I am disappointed that someone would believe it to be true (otherwise why say it?) and not bother to ask me about it in an attempt to determine the truth. Whoever made the comment was uninformed and did not seek to be informed. My guess is that this all resulted from an inquiry made by my secretary and that her inquiry was then attributed to me. (I, however, am not aware of any such inquiry.) In any event, whoever made the statement was, at best, reckless.

The response? Nothing. No apology. Nothing.

CHAPTER 22

Find Humor

● ● ●

I REMEMBER WHEN I TOOK my youngest daughter, Jessie, to a Goodwill Games match when she was six. It was women's indoor field hockey or something similar. One of the teams was from an Asian country; I don't recall exactly which one. But Jessie was intrigued. She stared at the Asian team as the women moved up and down the field, turning to me from time to time with a puzzled look. She spoke no words as she watched. Finally, putting two and two together in her mind, she turned to me and exclaimed, "They are all twins!"

One evening in the office, I heard someone running down the hall as I sat at my desk. I didn't know at that moment, but I soon learned that the footsteps belonged to one of my partners in search of another of our partners, whose last name happened to be White. The running partner flew into my office, saw me, stopped in his tracks, and without thinking, exclaimed, "You're not White!"

I stared at my partner for a moment and then said, "This is true. You are just now realizing this?" I paused for effect and then added, "Do you have a problem with that?" As the double meaning of his exclamation dawned on him, we both had a good laugh.

As I was boarding an Alaska Airlines flight, the captain was standing at the door. He was African American. I whispered to him, "If you are flying this plane, I'm not going." We shared a knowing chuckle. He went on to take his seat in the cockpit, and I took my seat in first class. Progress.

A white friend of mine, shortly after Obama was first elected president, told me how disappointed he was in me. He explained that all that time, he had thought that I wasn't president yet because the country would never elect an African American. Now, so he said, he saw me for what I was: an underachiever.

My long-time friend and legal assistant, Ellen Welichko, once received a box of chocolates from a client. As I walked by her office, she wanted to offer me a piece and called out. Unintended, her shout came out as, "Hey, chocolate!" I gave her the look and asked, "What did you call me?" We had a good laugh.

I was staying at a posh resort in Hawaii with my wife when, by coincidence, one of my best friends arrived. It just so happens that he is Jewish. We bumped into each other as he was being driven to his room in one of the resort carts by an African American employee. Understand that the room rates at this hotel are astronomical. He saw me walking along and exclaimed, "Oh, look! There's an

African American!" The look of OMG shock on the employee's face was priceless.

After starting Orrick's Seattle office, I called Roger Tolbert, one of my Perkins partners, to see if he would be willing to join me at Orrick. Roger is white. He thought it was a great idea. Caught up in the moment, Roger exclaimed, without thinking, that he and I went together like chocolate and peanut butter! "Which one of us is chocolate?" I asked.

I suppose we can choose to cry or be angry, but I would prefer to smile. America is so screwed up when it comes to race, but it doesn't have to be. All of us need to do a better job of laughing at ourselves and our common predicament. We will not solve our race puzzle without open and honest discussion, which cannot occur as long as barriers are in place—mental, physical, and social—serving to block acknowledgment and communication. One of the best ways to break down barriers is through humor. It makes it easier to talk about difficult subjects. As always, judgment is required, but perfection isn't. Maybe your first few swings will be awkward, but you will get the hang of it. It is simple, really. Fundamentally, you have to take the position that race doesn't matter, because, other than in appreciating diversity, it doesn't. You have to say it and you have to mean it and you have to live it. If you do, everything else will fall into place.

EPILOGUE

• • •

AT TIMES OVER THE YEARS, I have been treated unfairly at my law firms and elsewhere, and on more than one occasion, racism has played a part. But on which occasions? There are the blatant incidents, but no minority can know in the aggregate how many times he or she is adversely affected by racism—so much is silent, unspoken, anonymous. Furthermore, no minority can know how many times he or she mistook certain actions as racially motivated when they were not. As a minority, except in extreme cases, you are simply left to wonder.

There also have been times when I have been treated with generosity. The point of this book is not that the world is an awful place where things never go right but that institutional racism is a virus that is alive and well and needs to be eradicated if fundamental fairness is to be achieved. Black lives matter, and we must take issue and demand change, whether those lives are literally snuffed out in the blink of an eye or figuratively snuffed out in the polite confines of corporate America as the result of a thousand cuts meted out over a period of years.

At major corporate institutions today and in most of our society, racism has gone underground. It is more sophisticated than the blatant bigotry of the past, cleverly hidden from view but still highly effective. The resulting burdens placed on minorities in corporate America continue to inflict extraordinary strain on the mind and body. It would be naïve to think that the pressures never adversely impact minority performance, amplifying the effects of bias, unconscious and otherwise. Achieving success in this environment takes hard work, determination, courage, and discipline at levels not expected of or required of the majority. Giving up might be justified, but we do not give up, and, with determination and the support of others, we keep our perspectives and live to triumph.

We have learned to deal with a sometimes harsh reality, understanding that while there are many things we cannot control, we can control what is most important. We can control how hard we work and how well we live and the extent to which we are willing to persevere in the face of hardship and challenge. We can control whether we fight on or give up. We can control whether we are honest or betray the trust of others, whether we love or hate. We can control the depth of our integrity and whether we treat others with respect. We can control whether we give to others or wallow in self-pity, whether we are always loyal or loyal only when it is convenient. We have choices.

Although it is unlikely that we will ever get everything we wish for or work for or deserve, and while the ultimate level of our success and happiness might be tempered by forces beyond our control, in a very real sense, whether we succeed or fail, survive or die, is entirely up to us.

The problems I describe are very real and seemingly intractable. Their complete resolution is decades away. Undoing over three hundred years of institutionalized racism takes time. We have waited for centuries to see the promise of full equality realized in America, and we will be waiting decades more before prejudice and bias are erased as a practical matter. That said, racism can never be used as an excuse for not succeeding in America. Racism may stand in the way of achieving a precise objective, but only the individual can stop himself or herself from achieving fundamental success. We all must accept our reality and, frankly, deal with it.

This is not to say, however, that we shouldn't work hard to correct what needs correcting. We as a society must acknowledge the bias that stubbornly refuses to die and its effect on minority populations, doing our part to truly level the playing field. Only then may we hope to see America complete its long, slow march to honest and enduring equality.

Made in the USA
Las Vegas, NV
18 February 2021